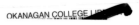

# Ride the Wind, Choose the Fire

## A Journey with Joan of Arc

## By

# Veronica Schwarz

Ride the Wind, Choose the Fire

A copy of this publication can be found in the National Library of Australia.

Edition: 1st
ISBN:  978-1-921681-40-0 (pbk.)

Published by Book Pal
www.bookpal.com.au

.

PO Box 3422
Sunnybank Hills LPO
QLD 4109

# Contents

# Foreword

Why would anyone write another book about Joan of Arc?

There are thousands of books, numerous movies and countless websites about her.

In spite of that, I felt inspired to write this particular book for a number of reasons.

I wanted to make Joan's story accessible to people of all ages who might not usually read history but would find these interviews (imaginary as they are) an easier way into her amazing but short life. I also hope that teachers will direct their students to this story as its accuracy is based on many years of research and several trips to France.

This work is a salute to and a celebration of one of the most amazing human beings of all time. Brave beyond belief on the battle field, stoic when wounded repeatedly, gentle and compassionate, staunchly loyal even in the face of betrayal. She died horribly when she was only nineteen and yet she is a role model of faith, persistence, devotion and courage.

My aim is to keep Joan's memory alive, not as a saint or a superwoman with extraordinary powers but as a wonderful human being with the same fears and pain and frustrations as the rest of us. A human being who steadfastly stuck to her purpose and showed us what belief and commitment can achieve.

To the friends and family members who supported me through this long project, my sincere thanks. It helped immensely knowing that you were cheering me on.

My thanks to my friends Olive Stonyer and Suzanne Pinchen, for their invaluable help with proofreading. Any errors remaining are solely mine, made in the final moments of completion.

For the courage to write a creative non-fiction version of Joan's life, I am grateful to Mark Twain, Bernard Shaw and Tom Kenneally.

Above all, Joan the Maid, I salute you. This book is for you.

*Veronica Schwarz*

# Pronunciation Guide

There are quite a few differences in pronunciation between French and English, and French has many nasal sounds.

This section does not try to give you a total outline of French pronunciation but mainly covers sounds in the names or words you will read in the book.

One major difference occurs when the very last letter in a word is a consonant. It is not pronounced. For example, Denis is pronounced in French as duh-nee. No *s* on the end. One major exception to this is the letter *c* so Joan's family name *d'Arc* is pronounced *dark*. The word for Duke, *duc* is pronounced *dook*. The *oo* sound is not exactly like *oo* in English. Hold your lips as though you are about to say *oo* and say *ee* instead. Now try saying *duc*.

The letter *j* is pronounced the same as *s* in the English word *pleasure*.

The vowel *a* is pronounced the same as it is in the English word *apple* except when it is written *â*. Then it is pronounced *ah*. So Joan's name is *Jeanne d'Arc* is pronounced *jan dark* in French, making sure you get that *j* sounding like the *s* in *pleasure*.

The nasal sounds are better listened to rather than described but the following will give you some idea.

The letters *m* and *n* after certain vowels are not pronounced at all in French. To say these sounds, pretend you have a bad cold and your nose is blocked. Now try saying *n*. The *m* is pronounced the same as the *n*. In the list below, this sound is shown by a black dot.

| | | | |
|---|---|---|---|
| Alençon | A-lo•-so• | La Pucelle | la poo-sel |
| Augustins | oh-goo-sta• | Loire | lwah |
| Beau duc | boh dook | Neufchateau | nerf-shat-oh |
| Beaugency | boh-jo•- see | Orléans. | or-lay-o• |
| Beauvais | boh-vay | Pierre | pee-air |
| Cauchon | koh-sho• | Poitiers | pwah-tee-ay |
| Chinon | shee-no• | Pucelle | poo-sel |
| Compiègne | kom-pee-en-yuh | Reims | ra•s |
| Dauphin | doh-fa• | Robert de Baudricourt | ro-bair duh boh-dree-koor |
| Domremy | do•-ray-mee | Rouen | roo-o• |
| Dunois | doo-nwa | Saint Denis | sa• duh-nee |
| Durand Laxart | doo-ro• laks-ar | Saint Loup | sa• loo |
| Fierbois | fee-air-bwa | Saint Ouen | s• too-o• |
| Isabeau | ee-za-boh | Seine | sayn |
| Jacques d'Arc | jak dark | Tourelles | too-rel |
| Jargeau | jah-joh | Vaucouleurs | voh-koo-ler |
| Jean Lemaitre | jo• luh-maytr | | |
| Jeanne | jarn | | |
| Jeannette | jarn-et | | |
| La Hire | la eer | | |

# The Maid

She was going to die and more than ten thousand people had come to watch.

The rumbling cart carried her into the town square and the crowd stirred like a huge beast turning towards her. A roar went up, then all was quiet. Necks craned to see her. Men hoisted small children onto their shoulders to make sure they could see her too.

And what did they see? A young woman weeping with terror, supported by two priests. Her head was shaven and she wore a shapeless dress of rough black cloth.

Three platforms had been built in the centre of the town square. On one, officials and churchmen in their finest robes of red velvet, ermine and silk, sat on chairs placed especially for the occasion. They would miss nothing.

On the second platform, a lone churchman stood, ready with his sermon and his judgment.

The third platform held a tall stake. Firewood leant against it, piled high.

No one would miss her death. The stake had been built so high even the executioner would be unable to reach her to strangle her mercifully. She would die in the fire.

The place was Rouen, in France. The year: 1431.

What had she done to earn so much hate? She was only nineteen. Hardly time to stir up such feelings in so many.

And now, she's been dead for nearly six hundred years.

So much was recorded from the time when she lived that we can piece it together. Come with me on a remarkable journey through time and place as I "interview" one of the most amazing people who ever lived – Jeanne d'Arc or Joan of

*Arc as she is known in English - Joan the Maid as she called herself.*

*My journey with Joan began when I visited the small town of Domremy, her birthplace. The town has been re-named Domremy-la-Pucelle after Joan's chosen surname "la Pucelle", meaning the Maid*

.

# SECTION I: DOMREMY

*France in 1429*
*Joan's birthplace, Domremy, is marked with a star.*

# Chapter 1: Getting There

Getting to Domremy without a car proved complicated but I was determined. I figured if Joan could criss cross France on horseback, I could get myself to Domremy. A train trip from Paris to Nancy then a regional train to Neufchateau and a two-hour wait for a bus. By the time the bus got to Domremy, I was the only passenger. My French grew more fluent as I chatted to the driver and told him I was interested in Jeanne d'Arc. As he stopped the bus for me to get out, he pointed to a small church on his right.

"Start here. I'll be back in four hours for the return trip."

I stood in the middle of the dusty road as he drove off. The air was dense and dry; the sun was hot on my skin. There was no breeze. Shading my eyes against the glare, I looked at the small stone church. It had been built in the fourteenth century and remodeled in the sixteenth. Joan of Arc took her first Communion here around 1423.

*The church at Domremy.*
*To the right, is a statue symbolising France giving Joan*
*a sword.*

I walked across the road and into the church. As my eyes adjusted to the dark, I felt the peace and calm of this tiny place. The air was cool. I had the place to myself so I sat on a pew, soaked in the atmosphere and looked at the beautiful stained glass windows. The brilliant colours showed scenes from the last few years of Joan's life. The story started at the back on the left and continuing clockwise to the front of the church and then up the right-hand side to the back of the church. The final scene on the left showed, in vivid colour, a young woman chained to a stake, burning to death.

Aloud, I asked, 'If you knew how it was going to end, would you have begun at all?'

In my mind, an answer formed. Perhaps it was imagination. Perhaps it was wishful thinking.

'You deserve to be better known,' I said. 'Many people have heard of you but few know the amazing details.'

*Stained glass window in the church at Domremy*

It was then I decided to put together the mountain of information available about her and record it as a series of imaginary interviews.

I left the church and walked into the dazzling sunlight of Domremy in May. Momentarily blinded after the cool darkness, I paused and looked back at the church. In the nineteenth century, the original altar was removed and the nave destroyed to make way for the road on which I stood. The original steeple was left standing and a new nave and altar built behind it. This means that the steeple is now at the front of the church. Back to front from when Joan knew it.

The air was hot and heavy. Nothing stirred as I wandered across the dusty street to a small tavern. To the right was a souvenir shop so I detoured in and bought a couple of souvenirs of Joan of Arc – a postcard and a small poem.

The poem *Fumées et Cendres* (Smoke and Ashes) by Andrée Nex gave powerful sound and life to the image in that last stained glass window. The fear, the horror, the savagery and the loss. As Joan's defenceless body is turned to a charred carcass in Rouen. The last verse reads:

> *Et pour toujours,*
> *Un cri*
> *Un cri d'honneur*
> *Du corps devenu carcasse*
> *De Jehanne, en place de Rouen.*

And forever, a cry. A cry of honour. Of body turned to carcass. Of Joan, in Rouen's marketplace.

Almost gasping for breath at the horror of it, I left the souvenir shop and, returning to the sidewalk, I sat at one of the tables outside the tavern. A waitress appeared and I ordered a *pichon* of white wine.

I had three hours to wait for the next bus out of Domremy. Plenty of time to look around the village but first I wanted to think about Joan and my sense of a mission to bring her back into the minds – and perhaps the hearts – of as many people as possible.

It's said we need heroes and I think that's true. Here is one of the greatest of heroes and perhaps one of the most amazing human beings of all time. Mark Twain wrote a book about her and considered it the best thing he had ever written. Most of his readers are unaware of the book about Joan but love Tom Sawyer and Huck Finn, two fictional boys.

Bernard Shaw wrote a play about her. In his preface, he summed up the amazing and the paradoxical. He wrote:

> *She is the most notable Warrior Saint in the Christian calendar... Though a professed and most pious Catholic ... she was in fact one of the first Protestant martyrs. She was also one of the first apostles of Nationalism, and the first French practitioner of Napoleonic realism in warfare as distinguished from the sporting ransom-gambling chivalry of her times. She was the pioneer of rational dressing for women ...*

> *It is hardly surprising,* he continues, *that she was judicially burnt, ostensibly for a number of*

*crimes,... but essentially for what we call unwomanly
and insufferable presumption. [1]*

I pulled myself back to the present. I had finally
made it to Joan's birthplace.

This small village is in Lorraine, one of the twenty-
six Regions of France. It is the only French Region to
have borders with three other countries – Germany,
Belgium and Luxembourg. As the crossroads of four
nations, it was a strategic asset to whichever of them
possessed it. But beyond this fact, it had given birth to a
nation's hero, one whose name is recognised in most of
the Western world – Joan of Arc.

The small village gave no sign of its reflected
greatness as it dozed in the sun. The heat and glare
grew stronger and I moved to the shade of a large
umbrella over one of the other tables. I sipped a little
more of the wine, still refreshingly cool in its earthen-
ware jug. I felt myself relax. Taking a deep breath I
wrote the words 'Hello Joan. Bonjour Jeanne,' in my
notebook.

In the glaring heat of the afternoon, my imagination began to work and I continued to write. What
follows is a record of a series of imaginary interviews
over a long period of time, interviews with Joan of Arc -
- as she might have told her story.

'I'm glad to hear from you,' said a voice in my
head. 'What are you doing?'

---

[1] Shaw, Bernard. *Saint Joan.* Penguin Books, Mitcham, Vic.
1955

The page of my notebook fluttered slightly as if a breeze stirred it. But there was none. I wrote: 'I want to write your story "as told by you". Will you help me?'

'Well, it wouldn't be "as told by me" if I don't.'

I could see immediately why her judges had found her difficult and far from diffident when they were questioning her. 'True,' I said. 'Lots of people have written about you of course. There's enough recorded material.'

The voice in my head answered, 'Then let's do it.'

Just what I wanted to hear. 'Terrific,' I said. 'Let's just clear up something about your voice and language. You don't sound much like a fifteenth century maid – and you're speaking English.'

I thought I heard her laugh: 'After what I've been through, your voice would change too. Dead at nineteen. That was a rude shock.'

'And the English language?'

'Well, in my situation, I can afford to be flexible. This reminds me how those learned judges and the English could not believe that St Catherine, St Margaret and St Michael spoke to me in French! They assumed all saints spoke only English!'

'Okay,' I said. 'I'm glad we cleared that up. So what or where will we start about those nineteen years?'

'My most vivid memory is the fire. You try putting your feet in a fire and gazing to heaven. Neither good for the Soul nor the soles. Those artists and film makers must be crazy or stupid or both, depicting me with a blissful expression gazing up to heaven while I'm being roasted alive. I still shudder at the thought. Let's talk about something else.'

A shudder ran through me too. Death by fire is fairly high on the list of everybody's major fears. I had read enough to know that her death had been particularly gruesome with even the executioner beside himself with grief and remorse.

She spoke clearly and with little trace of an accent. But perhaps I'm dreaming. I'm hearing voices in my head. No make that one voice. I'm hearing the voice of a girl who heard voices.

'Do you mind if I call you Joan?' I asked. 'It's what we call you in English.'

'I prefer Jeanne but if it's easier for you, call me Joan.'

'Thanks,' I said. 'You are called Jeanne d'Arc in history but that wasn't your name was it? Later writers, following the custom of their own time period, have given you that surname because it was your father's surname. You were never Joan "of Arc" When your trial judges asked you to state your names and surnames (yes, plural), you answered:

> *In my town they called me Jeannette, and since I came to France I have been called Joan. As for my surname, I know of none.*[2]

---

[2] Pernoud, Régine, *Joan of Arc*, Scarborough House, London, 1982, p. 15

'That's true,' she replied. 'In the area I lived, children were more often given their mother's surname than their father's. Or a combination of the two parents or something different again. Sometimes the surname was relevant to the place a person was born in, or even the work they did. Once my mission began I called myself simply Jeanne the Maid. The French word for "maid" or "maiden" in the sense of being a virgin is "pucelle". I was usually referred to as "La Pucelle", the Maid. Later when the King ennobled my family, we were all given the surname du Lys. My brothers chose to use it. I did not. I continued to call myself The Maid.

'Thanks,' I said. 'Joan, one of the things you're best known for is that you heard voices telling you to do amazing things for France. Can you tell me about those voices?'

There was a long silence and I wondered if I had lost her. I remembered she had not wanted to discuss her voices when her judges questioned her at her trial. Had I ended our talks before they had begun?

# Chapter 2: Giving Voice to Joan

At last, I heard her voice: 'What would you like to know?'

Delighted that she had chosen to respond, I asked, 'When did you first hear the voices?'

'The first time – it was in 1425 - I was about twelve. It was quite near our house in my father's garden. I'll show you the spot later. No one else was around. It was almost midday and hot. A bit like today actually.

'I heard "Jeanne. Jeanne." At first I was afraid. The voice was coming from the right hand side towards the church over there. There was also a brightness on that side.'

The date struck me. It was the year that the Burgundians raided the village and burnt the church. It would have been a tremendous shock to all the village not least of all a young girl on the verge of puberty. I wondered if this had made her vulnerable to hoping for divine assistance but I did not want to distract her at this point.

'What did the voice say?' I asked.

'Nothing much in the beginning. But I began to hear it quite regularly. It told me to be a good child and to go to church regularly. It also told me that God would look after me.'

'Whose voice was that?'

'I believed from the things he said that it was the Archangel Michael. After a while he told me that St Catherine and St Margaret would also advise me and I should listen to what they said.'

'The voices were with you constantly for almost five years before you were able to do what they said to help France and the King.'

'Yes and they remained with me for the rest of my life.'

*Not that that was long,* I thought.

Aloud I said 'There are many who believe your voices were a common mental problem. What would you say to that?'

'They were very clear and always helpful. So all I can say is they were very real to me. They began to tell me that I should go into France. They told me of the state of the war there and said that I must help the King of France.'

'Weren't you born in France? Wasn't Domremy part of France?'

'Yes and no. Things were different then. I'll draw you a map later. But to get back to my voices. They told me I must raise the siege of Orléans but I was not to tell my father what I was doing. I replied that, since I was only a girl, I couldn't even ride a horse let alone lead an army.'

'Did you tell anyone about the voices?'

'No, not for quite a while.'

'Right. Let's go back a bit. Tell us about your childhood.'

'Fairly ordinary for the time. My mother and father lived here in Domremy. As you know, nowadays it's not far from the German border. Of course, there was no such thing as Germany back then. For that matter, there wasn't much of a Kingdom of France either.'

I interrupted her. 'I want to get back to the geography and politics of it all a little later but, for now, can you tell me about your family.'

Although I could not see her, she seemed to take my interruption in her stride and answered 'Our house is over there still, on the other side of the church. The church used to face the other way in those days.

'My father was Jacques d'Arc. He came from Ceffonds, a village in Champagne. He was an important person in Domremy, being lower in rank only to the mayor and the sheriff. He represented the village on a couple of occasions in legal matters.'

'How did you get on with your father?' I asked.

'He kept me under his thumb especially after the dream he had about me. I'll tell you about that when we get to it.'

'All right,' I said. 'Tell me about your mother.'

'My mother was Isabelle Romée or Isabelle de Vouthon. Romée is a surname usually given to people who've made a pilgrimage to Rome or some other important pilgrimage.'

'Had she?' I asked.

'I don't think she ever got to Rome but she had gone on at least one pilgrimage to Puy-en-Velay. When she was sixty years old and Papa was dead, she started the appeal to the Pope to re-examine my trial. Imagine it, a peasant and a mere woman, in the fifteenth century, tackling the Pope in faraway Rome, to rehabilitate her dead daughter.'

'I begin to see where you got some of your characteristics. Tell me what your life was like. Were you different from the other children?'

'No. I didn't think so. I did go to confession and Communion more than most. The other children teased me a bit for being overly religious. I helped around the house. I was very good at spinning. I was also able to wander off and spend time on my own a bit.'

'Did you learn to read and write?'

'No. Most people didn't. I never learned to write but I could recognise some of the letters and words I saw in the church. Later on, I learnt to write my name. Jehanne. That's how it was spelt in French in those days. Nowadays, it's written as Jeanne.'

*Joan's signature*

'How much did you know of the politics of the time, the battles and the war with England?'

'Not a lot to be honest,' Joan answered. 'We were raided by the Burgundians a couple of times and had to escape to shelter for a few days. Sometimes, we'd have one of our soldiers come through the village. We listened to their stories and gave them food. Sometimes they'd stay overnight and I'd let them have my bed.'

'So where did you sleep when that happened?'

'Usually under the hood of the fireplace. Anyway, they were our main source of news. Quite a bit different to your day, eh! Now you can sit at home and watch a war on the other side of the world as it's happening.'

'Yes,' I admitted. 'It has become a lot more part of our lives without actually being part of our lives.'

Joan went on. 'There was also talk of the need for the Dauphin Charles, or crown prince as you would call him, to be crowned in the cathedral at Reims[3].

'The voices kept telling me that I was the one to do it. Now, believe me, that was a shock. Up until then I was just an ordinary sort of a girl. After I began to hear those voices, I dedicated myself to God and made up my mind to remain a virgin and never get married. Meanwhile, the voices continued to tell me to help the Dauphin.'

I said nothing so she continued.

'I asked the voices: "How, how can it be done?"

"Go to the Dauphin. Tell him you are sent by God," they replied. "Go to him. We'll help you. Just go."

'The voice of St Michael told me to go to Robert de Baudricourt for an escort. He was the King's representative in our area and he was stationed in Vaucouleurs.

'Just go! Easy for them to say. I didn't even know where Charles was. I'd never been far from Domremy. I

---

[3] I have used the French spelling of place names throughout. VS

had no idea where towns like Reims were. They were just names. I had no idea of distances and I've mentioned already that I couldn't even ride a horse. When I think about it now, the whole idea seems laughable. How true it is that ignorance is bliss.

'If I'd known all the hurdles, perhaps I'd have realised it was impossible and common sense would have prevailed. But I didn't know it was impossible so I just did it. Funny isn't it?'

When I thought of that last stained glass window and the way it all ended for Joan, I didn't think it was funny at all. I changed the subject.

'I guess it's time to find out what the problem was. Why were the English invading France? Why couldn't the King of France just get crowned and be done with it? Why did France need Joan of Arc?'

# Chapter 3: Let's You and Him Fight

She repeated my question amending the surname. 'Why did France need Jeanne the Maid?'

Her voice was clear, soft and feminine just as her friends and family had described it. I still could not see her. 'Walk to the bridge over the river,' her voice said.

I packed up my notebook, swallowed the last of the wine and walked along the deserted road. I passed the church and the house of Joan of Arc on my right and headed towards the bridge. *I'll visit the house later*, I promised myself.

I followed the road as it curved round to the left and walked towards the tall white statue that stands near the bridge. The statue depicts the young, innocent peasant girl beside the figure of a woman who symbolises France. The tall woman is handing Joan a sword and whispering to her that she must use it to save France.

*France giving Joan a sword*

I reached the statue and walked around it to look up at the two figures. I hadn't heard Joan's voice since I left the tavern so I wasn't sure if she was still with me.

'What do you think of this?' I asked, pointing to the statue.

To my relief, she answered. 'Just a moment. I'll have to have a look at it.'

'What do you mean? Haven't you seen it before?'

'I really haven't been back here much. Just had a wander through the house once and that was it. I wanted to feel my home and my mother again. No – I haven't had a look at this statue. It's certainly pretty and hey, don't I look sweet!'

In my mind's eye, I was suddenly sure I could see her. She stood in front of me looking up at the statue. I wanted to reach out and touch her to see if she was real but my hands stayed by my sides. I felt it would be intrusive but I also feared proving there was no one there. As I continued to look at her, her presence grew stronger. She turned and smiled at me.

'Ah, I guess you can see me now,' she said as though it were the most ordinary thing in the world.

She was dressed like a page boy and at first I thought her outfit was black. As she moved, I realized it was rich velvet in the deepest purple. It was so beautiful that I longed to reach out and touch it. But again, I did not.

She had referred to the appearance of the statue as sweet but my mind had brought her to life for me. She was there in front of my eyes. Short dark hair cut in a page boy bob, straight all around just above her shoulders. She had large brown eyes, a plain but strong face, a short figure with full breasts and strong legs. I recalled that there were no portraits of her done in her lifetime and all we have is hearsay - and a black hair placed in her wax seal. It was the custom then to include a strand of one's hair in the seal of a letter. So the only definite thing we know is that she had black hair. We also have the descriptions given by her family and friends.

I beckoned to her to come and stand on the bridge. She walked beside me and we stood together looking across the few metres of the river.

'What difference did this river make?' I asked.

'This river! Well, it was complicated. Domremy was a crossroads and a boundary - It was a political minefield. Now there's a modern warfare term your lot can be less than proud of.'

'I agree about the landmines, I said. 'Diabolical. Some people are working on banning them. But banning any effective weapon is like trying to separate a dog from its bark.'

'Or its bite! We used to have things called caltrops. Not deadly like landmines but they could do a bit of damage. Nasty iron pointed things. No matter how they lay, they had a point sticking upwards. Dreadful for foot soldiers and horses. I stood on one myself once.

*A caltrop from the time of Joan*

Let's sit down under the tree over there and I'll try and tell you the complex story of Domremy and of France.'

We walked back towards the statue, crossed the road and sat under a shady laurel. A map of Domremy and surroundings had been painted on a board nearby. Joan looked at the map and thought for a while. I could see her quite clearly now.

'Have you heard of the Hundred Years War?' she asked.

'Yes, but a hundred years seems a ridiculous time to run a war,' I replied.

'It really did go on for one hundred years and a bit more,' she said. 'It was a war mainly conducted by the English kings because they tried to unite the kingdoms of France and England under their rule. Have you heard of William of Normandy, William the Conqueror you call him?'

I nodded. 'Yes – Ten sixty-six and all that,' I replied, remembering the wonderfully funny book of the same name.

She smiled then her face grew serious and she continued the history lesson.

'Anyway, ever since William the Conqueror crossed over from Normandy in northern France, and conquered England in 1066, English kings ruled in England as well as Normandy. That was the beginning of all the trouble.'

'So it all began with a French Duke taking over England,' I interrupted. 'It wasn't just the English trying to take over France.'

Joan sighed. 'True,' she said. 'That was nearly 350 years before I was born. It's all a bit convoluted so stick with me.

'Through various marriages over time, the English kings acquired more and more of France. These royal marriages not only complicated the ownership of land but also made it difficult to know who was heir to what. It all came to a head in 1328 when the King of France died and the legitimate heir to the French throne was his grandson, the King of England. But the French refused to accept a king of England and gave the crown to the dead King's nephew.

'The English King Edward III decided he had the right to the kingdom of France. He invaded and that's when the Hundred Years War really got going.

'It was absolute chaos throughout most of France with constant battles and marauding soldiers ranging over the countryside. No one living could remember what peace had been like. Bands of soldiers, mercenaries really, roamed the countryside, taking what they wanted, raping women, destroying and stealing to make up for the fact that most of the time they were not paid. Where I lived was affected but not as badly as other parts of France.

'The French should have united and driven the English out but they fought against each other as well.

Not long before I was born, the King of France was Charles VI. He became quite insane and his wife Isabeau ran all his affairs. The two most powerful dukes in France, the Duke of Burgundy and the Duke of Orléans took advantage of the King's insanity to fight against each other for control of the kingdom. The Duke of Burgundy controlled mostly the north and east of the country and the Duke of Orléans controlled mostly the south.

'I'll draw you a map.' She cleared an area of the dry soil between us then she continued her story as she drew.

*A reconstructed map of France in 1428*

'Just five years before I was born, the Duke of Burgundy, John, joined with the English in an alliance against that part of France loyal to the Duke of Orléans and the King of France. John also organized the murder of his rival, the Duke of Orléans.' She indicated the two parts of France on her map. 'This part at the top of the map was loyal to the Duke of Burgundy and the English. There's another part down here near Spain that also belonged to the Duke of Burgundy. This middle section was loyal to Charles the Dauphin. So too was this tiny little part in the northeast with the towns of Domremy and Vaucouleurs.'

She pointed to the tiny island of land bordering Burgundian France and the Holy Roman Empire. That part of France where we were sitting.

She continued: 'The Duke of Orléans had married Anne of Armagnac and they had three young sons. After the murder of the Duke of Orléans, his father-in-law, Bernard d'Armagnac, took care of the sons and took control of the party supporting the Dauphin. This is how people on the side of the Duke of Orléans came to be called Armagnacs rather than Orléanists which would have made more sense.

'Anyway, things got worse. John of Burgundy, having killed the Duke of Orléans and formed an alliance with the English, then went to a meeting with the Dauphin. John of Burgundy was assassinated at this meeting. Nobody knows for sure if the Dauphin was involved but John's son, Philip, swore to get even with him. This was in 1419. I was about seven years old by then.

'Amazingly, Philip of Burgundy gained the support of Isabeau, the Dauphin's own mother and, in 1420, with the English king, Henry V, they drew up a treaty, the Treaty of Troyes. As I told you, the King of France was insane so he was not consulted. Another necessary bit of information was that Henry V was married to the Dauphin's sister Catherine. And ...'

I interrupted. 'Yes, that's the story behind Shakespeare's play *Henry V*. After the Battle of Agincourt in 1415, he marries Catherine....'

Joan looked as though she had just discovered something nasty on the sole of her shoe. She turned up her nose and I suddenly remembered that Shakespeare had written a very unflattering play about her, true to the English propaganda of the day.

I was suddenly afraid I had offended her and I held my breath hoping she would continue.

# Chapter 4: The Mother of all Wars

She continued without comment on the English Bard and his plays and I breathed again.

'It's hard to understand a mother betraying her own son in the way Isabeau did. Admittedly, she chose to support the side led by Henry, her pregnant daughter's husband. Her other daughter, Michelle was also married to Philip, the son of the Duke of Burgundy. So what was a poor mother to do? Two daughters on one side, one son on the other.'

'I'm betting she went with the most politically expedient,' I said.

Joan smiled. 'We'll never know why she did what she did. But the Treaty of Troyes was drawn up and signed. To add insult to injury, Isabeau declared that her son, the Dauphin, was illegitimate.

'The Treaty disinherited the Dauphin from any claim to the throne of France and named Henry V of England and his wife Catherine's unborn son (Isabeau's grandson) as heir to the throne of France.'

Again I interrupted. 'I'm sorry but this is all incredible. What a mess. These people were so inbred! How on earth did anyone keep up with it all?'

Joan laughed at my confusion but then turned serious. 'Believe me there were people who kept a very careful record of all of this. Heads could roll if you got it wrong. Over the centuries, including the twentieth century, it didn't get any better. Royal marriages were arranged not for love but for land acquisition or peace in our time or some other political reason including an appropriately "blue-blooded" heir. The twentieth-first century seems to be seeing some loosening up of the British monarchy's strict marriage rules and France hasn't got a reigning royal family at all since the guillotine ended their right to rule.'

'We had better get back to your time. So what happened after this Treaty of Troyes?'

'Two years later, both Henry V of England and Charles VI of France died within a few months of each other. By the Treaty of Troyes, this made Henry's nine-month old son King of England and of France. Since the baby could not rule until he grew up, Henry V's brother, the Duke of Bedford was made Regent of both France and England and ruled for his baby nephew. Bedford offered the Regency of France to the Duke of Burgundy but he declined.

'At the same time, there was still the Armagnac party under the Duke of Orléans. This Duke was the son of the one who was murdered by the Duke of Burgundy. The Armagnacs were loyal to the French line of Kings and supported the Dauphin in his claim to the throne.

'But the Duke of Orléans had been captured at the Battle of Agincourt and was held prisoner in London waiting to be ransomed. His half-brother, Dunois, the Bastard of Orléans, was capably managing his affairs until he returned. Meanwhile, the uncrowned King, my Dauphin, Charles VII, held power in parts of France and waged a half-hearted war against the combined forces of England and the Burgundians.'

Again she pointed to the two sections of the map.

'Joan,' I interrupted, 'My head is spinning. I hope there's not too much more.'

Joan looked as though she were enjoying herself and continued, 'I should add that Philip, Duke of Burgundy was a very powerful man. He was called the Grand Duke of the West because he didn't just rule over Burgundy, but over land from the Alps in the south to the North Sea including Flanders and nearly all present-day Belgium and Holland.'

I couldn't help commenting, 'The whole situation was obviously a disaster and why do all these people have the same names? It's very confusing to remember who is who. It's all mind-blowing. So this is where your mission comes in?'

'Yes. To get Charles crowned in Reims. To make him the legitimate ruler in the eyes of the people. As you can see from the map, Reims was in territory held by the Burgundians and the English. The Dauphin had his court in Chinon down here in the south so I had to cross enemy-held territory just to get to him.'

Pointing to the tiny section of land, she continued, 'Where we are now was not actually part of France. It's called Lorraine. Although it was on the edge of the Burgundian territory, it owed allegiance to the Armagnacs. It was like a tiny island out there on its own. That's why I said I had to go into France to reach the Dauphin.'

I looked at the tiny isolated section of land that was surrounded by enemy territory and marveled that it had produced a young girl who would set out to save the entire nation.

'But this town of Domremy was like a tiny version of France. Here's another map. This time, I'll show you the town and the area around it.'

She drew a curving line in the dirt to represent the river near us then continued speaking as she drew her map.

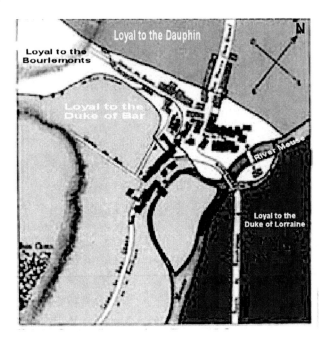

'Here's the river you see over there.'

She pointed to the right hand side of the map. 'It's called the Meuse. We are here and there's the bridge. The village was divided into two. Here to the left of us (she pointed down river), the land was in the Provostry of Montéclaire-Andelot and, therefore, was subject to the King of France.'

She saw my eyes glaze over and changed tack.

'I've tried to make it simple by dividing France into two camps but perhaps I should explain that it also was a cluster of groupings rather like a can of worms.

Various bits and pieces left over from the feudal system. They'd group and re-group, change loyalties and alliances to suit themselves. The whole thing was made even more complex by the territorial greed of various kings who should have kept their noses and their armies at home in England where they belonged. So that's about it. Are you sure you want all this detail?'

I thought about it and finally answered, 'I think so. It gives a snapshot of the complexities of politics that set out to destroy you. And the two maps help make it clearer. Anyone not interested can just skip over it. Okay. So back to Domremy. The land to the north of us owed its loyalty to the French crown. What about this section where we are at the southern end of the village?'

'It was controlled by the de Bourlément family who owed allegiance to the Duke of Bar who in turn owed allegiance to the Duke of Lorraine who supported the Burgundians who supported the English.'

I laughed. 'It sounds like …and this is the house that Jack built. What a tangle!'

Joan's puzzled look told me she had never heard the nursery rhyme about the house that Jack built.

She went on. 'Yes but that's how it was. It grew out of the feudal system, the seizure of land and the serfdom of the farmers and villagers.'

'Many people today don't have a clue what all that means. We don't seem to teach much history in our schools these days.'

'Well, we didn't have schools at all except for teaching boys in the monastery and private tuition for the sons of the aristocracy. Nothing for commoners or girls.'

'I know a lot has improved. So, about Domremy. More than half belonged to France and a small portion, your end of the village in fact, belonged to a series of masters whose allegiance belonged to the English and Burgundians.'

'That's right but it gets better. Or perhaps I should say worse. The heir to the Duchy of Bar was René d'Anjou. He had been on the pro-English side, but he actually joined my army and fought for the French side in the final campaigns.'

'We'll have to talk more about him later. What were the attitudes of the people in Domremy to the struggles of France against the Burgundians and the English? Were they divided like the village itself?'

'No – we were pretty much all for France. Not like that lot from over there.'

She thrust her chin out to indicate the other side of the river.

'What do you mean?'

'The villagers in Maxey. They were all for the Burgundians. Mind you, that side of the river was part of the Duchy of Lorraine and, like the land to the south of Domremy, had feudal ties to Burgundy anyway.'

'More patches in the patchwork quilt, eh?'

'Yes, I guess so but, as I said, we grew up with it and it all seemed pretty normal – most of the time.'

'Most of the time? What do you mean?'

'Well the boys from Domremy and Maxey would have a go at each other from time to time. You know how boys enjoy any excuse for a tussle. They'd brawl a bit but sometimes they'd have an all out go. Then they'd come home pretty bloody and battered.

'I mentioned before that we had been attacked at least twice that I could remember. There was an actual battle with soldiers just across the river there. It was when I was about thirteen, in midsummer; a band of Anglo-Burgundians burnt our church and drove off our cattle. That was one of our closest brushes with the war. Another time, about three years later, we were invaded again. The whole village had to run but that time we took our cattle with us. We sheltered in Neufchateau.'

Suddenly she changed the subject. 'That's enough history for one day. Let's go back to my parents' house. I know you want to have a look at it.'

I took one last look at the water under the bridge. How could such a small, peaceful river (well actually, where I come from we'd have called it a creek) have been the border marking so many divisions, local and national?

Then I walked back to the house of Joan of Arc.

# Chapter 5: Home is Where the Hearth Is

I retraced my steps from the river and the bridge and veered off to the left to visit the house of Joan of Arc. I have to admit, I could hardly believe my eyes. Whatever trees or garden had once surrounded it, were now gone and the house stood stark but elegant within its own space.

*Joan's house today.*

The exterior of the house is almost modern. For a start, it's two storeys high. The afternoon sun was gentler now and the plaster glowed with a cream tinge in the softer light. From the front, the left hand side is some two to three metres higher than the right, giving it an almost rakish modernistic slope. The two front windows, both upstairs and downstairs, are large and wooden framed. The right hand side wall of the house slopes away from the front at a very gentle angle which makes it appear to be part of the front wall with an eccentric little kink. A twentieth century architect would have been proud of it.

'What do you think of it?' she asked.

'Very impressive. I'm surprised at its size and style, I must admit. I expected something smaller and, no offence, more primitive.'

She laughed and clapped her hands. She was obviously delighted to have caused me some surprise. 'Let's go in and check it out,' she said, walking backwards towards the house and beckoning with both hands for me to follow her.

We walked through the front door and were immediately in the main room with its large fireplace to the left and the cool stone floor beneath our feet. I say large fireplace but it was the mantle that was huge. The actual hearth was quite average in size. The massive stone mantle jutted out from the wall. It stood a good one and a half metres above the tiled floor, supported by stone blocks sloping back to the wall at floor level. The room was empty and bare. Then I noticed the small bronze statue in the corner to our left, just beside the window.

It stood on a pedestal so that the small bronze face was level with mine. The figure was dressed in armour with a long skirt covering its legs. Precisely the con-straining style of clothing Joan had rejected. The artist, like so many others, had been unable to leave off this feminine touch.

*The small statue of Joan in her house. The enormous mantle piece is to the right.*

Joan walked up to the statue, held up the hem of her jacket with both hands and did a little soft shoe shuffle. I couldn't help laughing. She had spent time with knights and nobles, aristocratic ladies and a king but she still had her childlike sense of fun. (Even after months of imprisonment and questioning at her trial, she could still make a joke to the court officials.) She stopped her little dance, gave a small curtsy and turned to gaze at the bare fireplace. Her eyes were half closed and she stood very still.

'Such good times we used to have here. The fire would blaze at night and we'd gather round and tell stories or discuss local news and gossip. My mother always sat here and father sat over there.'

Abruptly, she turned from the fireplace and headed for the door opposite.

'Come and see the rest of the place,' she called over her shoulder.

We walked through the rooms on the ground floor. Joan pointed out the place where she slept and chattered happily like a small child. It was hard to keep up with her. The upstairs section of the house was closed off so we ended back in front of the fireplace. Joan walked over to the statue – the one thing that did not belong here. She stroked the bronze head gently.

'Well, little girl, would you have left here if you had known what they would do to you?' she whispered, her lips close to the bronze head.

The question hung in the air of the room. I had imagined the friendly warmth from the fireplace, the flames rising and falling, and the chatter and laughter of the family. But that question shattered the cosy picture and the imagined fire suddenly felt too hot for comfort.

We both headed for the door. Outside, we stood, not looking at each other. Finally Joan broke the silence.

'Over here is the place where I first heard the voice.'

She led me to our left to a low stone wall shaded by a tree that was too young to have been there when Joan had heard her first voice. There was a plaque on the stone wall informing me that this was indeed the place Joan of Arc first heard her voices. We sat down together on the stone wall. Joan's feet barely reached the ground.

*The spot near her house where Joan first heard the voice.*

The tree beside the wall cast its cool shade over us and, looking up into its branches, I said, 'At your trial, when the judges were trying to prove you were a witch, they put a lot of emphasis on a Fairy Tree near your village. What was that about?'

Joan's eyes grew dreamy as she remembered her childhood. 'There was a large old beech tree in the forest near here and, when I was a child, I'd go with the other girls of the village to hang garlands of flowers on its branches and dance near the tree. It was called The Tree of Ladies or The Fairy Tree. When I began to hear the voices, I stopped dancing at the Fairy Tree but I still sang there.

'Some people, particularly older ones claimed to have seen fairies in or near the tree. I never did. Next to the tree was a fountain and sometimes sick people would come to drink the water in the hope that it would cure them. Again, I never saw them cured but I did see them coming to the fountain to drink.

'All over the countryside at that time, people believed in magic, and spirits and fairies and the power of certain plants like mandrake. I didn't have any belief in it at all myself. I thought such things were sorcery and I had nothing to do with them.

'Some of the local nobles and their families would come to picnic under the tree or even join the villagers on special Sundays. It was all very harmless.'

She paused so I said, 'You've told me a bit about your father and mother. What about the rest of the family?'

I had a sister and three brothers. My eldest brother, Jacquemin, was grown up and living at Vouthon where Mama came from so I didn't have a lot to do with him. My second brother was Jean and my youngest brother Pierre was born a year after me. I had an older sister Catherine who married the son of the mayor of Greux, not far from Domremy. Sadly, she died before I left Domremy. Pierre and Jean came with me on my military campaigns but Jean didn't last long and left. Pierre stayed with me to the end and was captured with me at Compiègne.'

'I guess we'll hear more about him throughout the story. Tell me more about your father. Your relationship with him was a bit stormy at times though, wasn't it?'

'Yes, there were a couple of things that upset him even before I went away. One was the dream he had.'

'You were about fourteen at the time, weren't you and by then you had been hearing your voices for some two years.'

'Yes, I had. Papa never mentioned his dreams to me but Mama told me after he discussed them with her and my brothers. My brothers didn't mention them either. Papa told them he had dreamt that I would go away with soldiers. There was only one reason women followed the soldiers and Papa assumed his dream meant I would become a prostitute. He was so upset by this thought that he said to my brothers "If I believed that the thing I have dreamed of her should come to pass, I should want you to drown her; and if you did not do so, I would drown her myself"'.

'And three years later his dream came true but not in the way he thought. How do you explain it?'

'I can't.' she said simply

'Did this dream affect your father's attitude to you?'

'Very much. Both Papa and Mama became stricter with me and made sure I was under their or my older brother's supervision as much as possible.'

'What else upset your father?'

Joan sighed. 'He had organized a marriage for me but I had made a vow of chastity. I intended to remain a virgin and devote myself to the mission I had been given by the voices. Virginity was important in the religious atmosphere of the time as you'll understand when we get further on with the story. Anyway, I refused to marry. I admit it was unusual. Girls usually married someone their parents chose even if they didn't like them. The young man my father chose brought a breach of promise suit against me when I would not marry him but I swore to the judge that I had made no promise to him. Papa was furious.

'I knew he would not give up his efforts to marry me off and my determination to remain a virgin was obviously going to be a big stumbling block to a wedding. My voices had been speaking to me for almost five years, urging me to save France and crown the King. The pressure was becoming too great. I had to get on with my mission. There were at this time rumours of a renewed English attack on France so the political situation was also worsening.

'It was growing urgent. I had to obey my voices. I had to get to the Dauphin. According to the voices, the first step was to go to Vaucouleurs and get Robert de Baudricourt to give me an escort to ride into France to the royal court at Chinon. Sounds simple if you say it quickly.'

'Why did you need to see Robert de Baudricourt?'

'At the time, he was the governor at Vaucouleurs, a garrison town only twelve miles north of Domremy. This was the closest place held in the name of the Dauphin and Robert was the closest authority representing the Dauphin. I had to trust my voices but how could I do this with my father keeping a strict eye on me? And why would Robert de Baudricourt believe me, let alone help me?'

*Veronica Schwarz*

# SECTION 2: VAUCOULEURS

# Chapter 6: Home and Away

'The plan was simple. I had a cousin, also called Jeanne, or Joan as you would say. She lived near Vaucouleurs with her husband, Durand Lassois or Laxart as he is also known. He was sixteen years older than I so I called him Uncle out of respect.

'My voices told me to go to my Uncle Durand for help. It was May 1428, early summer, blossoms everywhere. I loved those May days. I never dreamed the last day I spent alive would be a day in May. I was full of life in those days and felt the urgency of my voices telling me to go, go, go. So, I asked my parents if I could visit Jeanne and Durand. It was horrible deceiving them like that but my voices came first.

'Mama and Papa agreed I could visit my cousin for a week.

'We had a lovely time together. Jeanne was gentle and kind and Uncle Durand made sure I had everything I needed. Towards the end of the week, I told my uncle about my mission to defeat the English and have the Dauphin crowned. He was the first person I told. He took it astonishingly well particularly when I reminded him of the prophecy that France would be lost through a woman and restored by a girl. I was sixteen at the time and he must have been shocked and surprised – even more so when I asked him to take me to Robert de Baudricourt for an escort to the Dauphin. But my voices were right. He agreed to help me.'

I interrupted. 'He must have admired and trusted you very much to put himself in such a position.'

'Yes, he was a wonderful support to me when I needed it right at the beginning. We arrived at Vaucouleurs and Uncle Durand lead the way to the room where Robert held audience and settled local disputes. There were other people standing around but I noticed one in particular who was watching me closely. I learned later that he was Bertrand de Poulengy, a man of noble birth, about thirty-eight years old, serving as an officer under Robert. He had visited my parents a number of times in Domremy so he knew of me although we had never met.

'Robert was the only one in the room who was seated, and when he beckoned to Uncle Durand and me, we stepped forward. Uncle Durand gave me a gentle encouraging push forward, then stepped back again to give me the floor. I stood there in my long red woollen dress looking like any other peasant girl Robert had ever seen so I guess it was a bit of a shock when he heard what I had to say.

'"I have come in the name of the Lord to ask you to send a message to the Dauphin," I said.'

'And what message is that?' he asked me.

"Tell the Dauphin to be careful and not to get involved in any battles because my Lord will give him help after mid-Lent. Also tell him that I will lead him to Reims to his coronation."'

'What on earth did Baudricourt say?' I asked.

'At first, he looked a bit startled then he slapped his thigh and burst out laughing. He was laughing so hard, there were tears in his eyes. Finally, he took control of himself and asked, "Who do you mean by your Lord?"

"The King of Heaven", I said straight away.

'He burst out laughing again and, looking at Uncle Durand, he said "Take this girl home to her family and tell her parents to give her a good thrashing. Now! Or I just might hand her over to my men for their pleasure. They could use a bit of light relief."

'So back we went to Uncle Durand's place, I said goodbye to Jeanne and headed home. Of course, Papa was furious and I was lucky to escape a beating. Life at home was pretty unpleasant for a while but bigger things were happening. Towards the end of July, the Burgundians were attacking towns near us and, as I mentioned earlier, we had to evacuate our village and shelter in the walled town of Neufchateau, taking all our cattle with us. My family and I stayed in the home of Madame La Rousse.'

'Your trial judges brought that up too, didn't they, accusing you of staying in a house of ill repute and even of working there?'

'Yes, they were really clutching at straws with that one. Can you imagine Mama and Papa staying in a brothel! And as for my working there, I helped Madame La Rousse with household chores while she had so many unexpected guests sheltering there.'

'Wasn't it here that a suitor took you to court for breach of promise?'

'Yes, we were only in Neufchateau two weeks and I had to go to Toul to answer the charge. The judge of the case concluded that I had made no such promise of marriage and dismissed the case.'

In Joan's time, a promise of marriage was considered a legally binding contract. It's possible that the man proprosed marriage and when Joan declined, he tried to revenge himself by taking her to court. Her parents were disappointed at the time as they would have preferred to see her married.

Joan continued, 'Of course, my trial judges brought this up too as an example of my bad behaviour. But let's pass on. When we returned to Domremy, we found the church in ruins and the village burned. Even then we were not safe and no one was allowed to wander outside the village. In addition, my parents seemed more determined than ever to get me married.

'In January 1429, I turned seventeen. It was definitely time to go. Uncle Durand's wife Jeanne was pregnant and I offered to go and help her. I left Domremy and, as it turned out, I never returned. It was an awful decision to have to make. My parents nearly went out of their minds when they found I had left them. I did not say a final goodbye to any one, although I knew I might never see them again. I simply said I was off to Vaucouleurs for a while. I did not wish to hurt them or make them sad. I felt as if my heart would break but I believed I had to do it.'

'Did you actually stay with Durand and Jeanne?'

'Yes. I did for several weeks. I travelled backward and forward from their village to Vaucouleurs where I stayed with friends of Uncle Durand's, Catherine and Henri le Royer. I also made a very interesting excursion to the town of Nancy during my stay.

'My main focus was to persuade Robert de Baudricourt to help me get to see the Dauphin. I seemed to be getting nowhere fast so I decided to head out on my own. I took some of Uncle Durand's clothes and dressed myself as a boy because that would be safer traveling across enemy territory and more practical for traveling. Uncle Durand and another man, Jacques Alaine came with me. We didn't get very far before I realised it was a mistake and turned back. I needed Robert's authority and a proper escort.

'Fortunately I was blessed to meet two men who helped me enormously.'

# Chapter 7: Clothes Maketh the Woman

'At Catherine and Henri's home, I met Jean de Nouillonpont, better known as Jean de Metz. He was about twenty-eight maybe thirty years of age and a gentleman, serving under Robert.'

I nodded. 'He was very impressed with you and gave a detailed report of your first meeting.'

I consulted my notes and continued: 'He told them

> *When Joan the Maid came to the place and town of Vaucouleurs, in the diocese of Toul, I saw her, dressed in poor clothes, women's clothes, red; she lodged at the house of one Henri Le Royer of Vaucouleurs. I spoke to her, saying "My dear girl, what are you doing here? Must it not be that the King be cast out of the kingdom and we all become English".[4]*

'According to him, you replied:

> *"I have come to this royal town to ask Robert de Baudricourt. either to lead or to send me under escort to the King. He takes no notice of me or of my words; nevertheless, before mid-Lent, I must be on my way to the King, even if I must wear out my legs to the knees. There is no one in the world, neither king, nor duke, nor daughter of the King of Scotland, nor any other who can regain the kingdom of France; there is*

---

[4] Pernoud, p. 35

*no help for the kingdom but in me. I would prefer to be spinning beside my poor mother, for these things do not belong to my station; yet it is necessary that I should go and do these things, since God wishes that I should do them."*

I drew a breath and I looked up from my notes. 'Did you really say all that?'

Joan smiled. 'It's a fairly accurate report. Yes.'

'What's the reference to the daughter of the King of Scotland?'

'The Dauphin's son Louis had just been betrothed to Margaret, daughter of the King of Scotland. Some people were hoping this new blood would give the French kingdom a fresh start.'

'So it seems that Jean de Metz was impressed with you immediately.'

'Yes. He took my hand and said, "I swear I will take you to the Dauphin myself. When do you want to leave?"

'I said "Better now than tomorrow and better tomorrow than later."

"And will you travel to see the Dauphin in this red dress you are now wearing?"

'He not only saw the impracticality of riding a horse for 350 miles in a dress but also the danger for a woman in a war zone.

"You are right," I said. "I will gladly wear men's clothes. It will be much safer and more practical on horseback."

'He later gave me clothes and boots which he borrowed from one of his men.'

This matter of Joan dressing in male clothing pre-occupied her trial judges and gave them the opportunity they were waiting for to condemn her to death. But the matter has also been much discussed by historians and writers since Joan's time.

We see that the idea was first suggested to her by Jean de Metz for very practical reasons. Similarly for practical reasons, Joan slept in full armour on the battlefield so as not to arouse any sexual interest in the men around her. She did this in spite of waking up very bruised as a result of sleeping in metal. When imprisoned and under constant threat of rape by her English guards, she was protected by the many layers and cords and lacings of her male hosen and jacket. A description of what she was wearing at the time she spent in prison, showed that her outfit contained almost double the cords and lacings of a normal outfit of the time. Her need to protect herself was very real and she wore the clothes appropriate to her circumstances.

She told her judges at her trial that she would wear female clothing if she were placed in the custody of the Church with a woman (usually a nun) with her, as was the custom. She complained several times that her guards were constantly trying to rape her but were unsuccessful while she wore her tightly laced male clothing. Even an English nobleman tried to rape her.

As I was thinking along these lines, Joan continued.

'The other man who helped me right at the beginning was Bertrand de Poulengy, who had been at my very first meeting with Robert de Baudricourt. Both he and Jean de Metz spoke to Robert on my behalf. But still he refused to send me to the Dauphin.'

I nodded. 'Joan, you mentioned that while you were in Vaucouleurs trying to persuade Robert de Baudricourt to give you an escort to the Dauphin, you made a trip to the town of Nancy to visit the Duke of Lorraine. Tell me about that. It seems unnecessary and a waste of time in the scheme of things. He was, after all, committed to the other side – the Burgundians and the English.'

# Chapter 8: Wives and Mistresses

'So why did you go to Nancy and talk to the Duke of Lorraine. It seems like a waste of time,' I repeated.

Joan shook her head. 'No, not such a waste of time because, as a result of that visit, his son-in-law, René, did join my army five months later. Anyway the Duke himself sent for me. I'd never been to Nancy, Charles of Lorraine was a Duke and he wanted to see me. So I went.

'He had a nasty dose of something he'd picked up while whoring and he was desperate enough to try anything. Apparently, he thought I could cure him.'

'And did you?'

Joan snorted. 'Of course not. I didn't perform magic -- or miracles either.'

'Some would say your whole performance in those last three years of your life was a miracle but what happened with the Duke. Was he angry, disappointed or how did he react to you?'

'At that stage, the only person of any real power and status I'd spoken to was Robert de Baudricourt. But when I got to Nancy and they took me to see Charles ....'

'Sorry to interrupt again but it's a bit confusing because the Dauphin was also a Charles. Perhaps you could just refer to this one by his title, Duke of Lorraine

'You're easily confused' she laughed. 'Don't you know any people with the same names?'

'Yes, but this is way in the past and vague figures in history ---'

'Vague figures! There was nothing vague about Charles of Lorraine. He had a wife whom he treated shamefully. Poor Margaret. And a mistress who lived next door and produced five children. Alison Dumay she was called. A harlot. Still, I felt sorry for her in the end. When Charles – that is, the Duke of Lorraine - died, the people of Nancy paraded her through the streets, pelting her with – er, how shall I say it – human excrement. Then they murdered her.'

I shuddered. 'Horrible. Being a mistress could be risky business especially once the benefactor dies or drops you. But, to get back to your visit to Nancy, what happened when you saw the Duke?'

'At first I thought he wanted to talk about my mission to crown the Dauphin in Reims and that perhaps he would change sides. It turned out that all he wanted to talk about was his health or, more to the point, his illness.

'I answered him straight up that I knew nothing about that but said if he'd give me some men, including his son-in-law René, to take into France, then I would pray for his health.'

'So you offered to pray for the duke's health in return for an escort into France, an escort which was to include René of Anjou the Duke's son-in-law. Why did you particularly ask for René?'

'He was quite an interesting and talented young man. He was related to Charles – I mean the Duke of Lorraine -- by marriage. René was only eleven when the Duke gave him his daughter in marriage. She was even younger. So, you see, René's loyalty to the English and the Burgundians was decided for him by a marriage and political alliance at an early age and not by any choice of his. I figured that getting him on side would be a good start to my mission. Old Sourpuss of Lorraine refused to allow it. I told him in no uncertain terms what I thought of his morals and his sex life and told him to go back to his wife. He took it pretty well actually and, to my surprise, gave me four francs and a black horse for my mission into France. Odd, eh? He was on the opposite side. The four francs wasn't much but it was a gesture and the horse even more so.'

'Why on earth would he do that?'

'I don't really know. At the time I thought it was because the angels were on my side but in hindsight, I think I was one of the few people who stood up to him and told him what I thought. Perhaps that impressed him.'

'You said earlier that René of Anjou joined your army later anyway. Can you tell me how he came to join you?'

'When René was still a minor, the Duke of Lorraine was his regent. That means he ran René's duchy for him till René was old enough to take over. When René did come of age, he showed he had a mind of his own and changed to the side fighting against the English. My side. Five months after my request for him to his father-in-law, Rene arrived in Reims for the coronation of the Dauphin and he stayed with me from then on. As I said, he was an interesting and talented young man. He was only twenty when he joined my army. He was a fine horseman, excellent with the lance, but he wrote poetry, illustrated books and loved tapestry. Not your usual young man at all.'

'Okay, so you left Nancy with four francs and a horse.'

# Chapter 9: Good or Evil?

'I rode back from Nancy to Vaucouleurs to check on Robert de Baudricourt and to stir him along a bit. The Duke of Lorraine was not going to equip me to go into France so it was time to put the pressure on Robert,' Joan continued her story.

'When was this?'

'It was February 12, 1429. I went straight to Baudricourt and told him that the Dauphin's army had suffered a defeat near Orléans that very day.'

'In those days, with no radio or other means of communication, how could you have known that?'

'I just did. It just came to me the way the voices did. Anyway, I told Robert there would be more defeats unless he sent me on my mission.'

'And did he?'

'No, not right away. The news of the defeat was brought to him by messenger a few days later. That's when he decided to sit up and take notice of me. That I had been right could not be denied. What he decided he needed to know was the source of my information. In those days, the only choice was between two sources – God or the Devil. So he decided to check my source.

'As I told you, I was staying at the home of Catherine le Royer in Vaucouleurs at the time. We both enjoyed spinning and were sitting together, chatting and spinning …'

'That's not a picture most people have of you, doing such a normal feminine thing.'

'Maybe not. But it's true. I loved to spin and was actually quite good at it.'

'Sorry to interrupt. It's just so different from the young-woman-on-the-horse-with-sword-in-hand image.'

'As I was saying, Catherine and I were spinning when Robert walked in with the local priest, Jean Fournier. The priest was wearing his stole and looking very serious indeed. Robert told Catherine to leave the room. I wondered what was going to happen next. This same priest had already heard my confession but he said to me "If you be an evil thing, keep back but if you are come from God, draw near".

'I walked slowly towards him and went down on my knees in front of him. They expected that, if I were an evil thing, a witch or possessed by the devil, I would have howled or writhed or foamed at the mouth or tried to escape when confronted by the priest and his stole. I knelt in front of the priest; I was so close that my face could have touched his robes.

'I glanced at Robert and saw the look on his face. A mixture of amazement and relief.

'I said to him "I must go to the Dauphin. Have you not heard the prophecy that France shall be lost through a woman and shall be redeemed by a virgin from the frontiers of Lorraine?"

'I was running out of time and had to push him into a decision you see. I felt like a woman ready to give birth. The time was urgent and the outcome unstoppable.

'Robert finally made up his mind. He sent a messenger with a letter to the Dauphin at Chinon telling him about me. After a bit of a wait, a messenger returned with a letter authorizing Robert to send me to the Court at Chinon. The messenger, Colet de Vienne, was told to escort me. Jean de Metz and Bertrand de Poulengy with their two servants also were to go with me. Oh, and Richard the Archer was part of the escort too.'

Her incredible memory after all that time amazed me but I said nothing. She had amazed her trial judges by correcting errors in reporting on her answers given days and weeks earlier that, when the records were checked, showed she was invariably correct.

She continued, 'I needed clothes and equipment for the journey and I was helped by many good people who already believed in me. The men who were to accompany me, de Metz and Poulengy, paid for most of it. Uncle Durand and some of the citizens who had grown to know me, also paid for some of my equipment. They bought me a man's black tunic, boots, spurs, and a horse. Robert de Baudricourt gave me a sword and I heard he did re-imburse Uncle Durand later.'

'What happened to the horse the Duke of Lorraine gave you?'

'It was not thought proper for me to ride to the Dauphin on a horse provided by a supporter of the English.'

Joan smiled and I could almost hear her practical mind singing – 'A horse is a horse, of course, of course.' But she did not say this. Sensitivities had to be observed and Joan had always been loyal to her friends and supporters even when they let her down.

'So you were finally on your way.'

Joan smiled happily. 'Yes, it was a great moment. Most of the townspeople came out to see us off. As we rode through the streets of Vaucouleurs, people waved and called out words of encouragement and blessing. It was a good start but what a journey! Three hundred and fifty miles, most of it in Anglo-Burgundian hands. 'We knew we could be attacked, robbed or killed if we were caught and rape was inevitable if any captors discovered I was a woman. The suggestion of my friends that I wear male clothing was a very wise one.'

I thought about Joan's later experiences at the hands of her English jailers and knew that rape was no fantasy for this young woman. I changed the subject.

*Veronica Schwarz*

# Chapter 10: Across Enemy Lines

'Vaucouleurs to Chinon. That's a bit over 560 kilometres. Nearly 350 miles. How long did it take you to ride that distance?'

'Eleven days as I recall. We set off in the late afternoon of 23 February 1429. Not a good time of year to travel but at least the snow was gone. Just cold and wet. Robert came out to send me on my way and he presented me with a sword as we were leaving. My hostess, Catherine le Royer came to wave goodbye as we headed out through the Porte de France.

'I wasn't used to horseback riding so I had to get used to that pretty quickly. My backside was covered with calluses by the end of it. We'd had a lot of heavy rain and all the rivers were overflowing their banks so that made for some interesting crossings. We crossed six rivers on the way and when the water was deep we had to swim the horses across. This meant we were wet and cold for a lot of the time but no one complained. We traveled mainly at night and I was happy to comply with Jean and Bertrand's decisions as to when to travel and when to hide and rest.'

I interrupted: 'You did keep trying to get them to let you hear Mass though, didn't you?'

'I did. But they only allowed it twice in the eleven days.'

I continued. 'Why wouldn't they let you hear Mass when you wanted to?'

'They were afraid I might be recognised if we went to any church in towns along the way.'

62

'So people had already heard of you and your mission even though you had done nothing spectacular up to that point?'

'Yes – word had begun to spread and since the prophecy about France being saved by a virgin from Lorraine was well known, many people wanted to believe I was the one.'

'You slept side by side with Jean and Bertrand during that journey and they both testified to their respect for you, such that neither of them felt any sexual desire for you. Bertrand even said:

> *I would never have dared to make her an evil proposal by reason of the virtue I divined in her."*

'Very unusual for soldiers of the time not to try to take advantage of the situation.'

Joan made no comment on this but continued with her story.

'As we rode, we talked about whether or not it was safe. Besides worrying about the dangers of the journey, the men were nervous about the sort of reception the Dauphin might give us when we reached Chinon. I assured them over and over that the Dauphin would welcome us. Jean de Metz asked me privately if I would really do the things I said I would. I told him that God and my brothers in Paradise had given me a mandate to recover the Kingdom of France.'

'That was a pretty tall order,' I commented. 'Not just for you to accomplish but for them to believe. You must have been very convincing.'

She nodded. 'I suppose I was because I totally believed it myself. I heard my voices often on that journey and I was completely confident.

'The first night after leaving Vaucouleurs, we traveled all night and reached St Urbain at daybreak. We stopped at the monastery and were given shelter by the Abbot. We traveled on to Auxerre and by then we were feeling more confident so they let me go to the cathedral to hear Mass. Thinking about it now, it probably wasn't all that clever. We could easily have been recognised but nothing happened and we continued on to Gien. Finally we crossed into territory that was controlled by the Dauphin. We were still not safe because, although there were no enemy soldiers there were still bands of robbers roaming the countryside, preying on travelers. This included the underpaid or even unpaid soldiers of the Dauphin.

'We were in fact ambushed after we left Gien. Some people have thought this was a trick that my own companions played on me but that doesn't make sense. With only so few of us, we'd have missed anyone who separated from the group and tried to pull such a prank. Besides, fun is fun but this was not the time for it. When we were confronted by a group of men, my escort wanted to run away but I told them not to be afraid, that the men would do us no harm. As it turned out, they moved away and left us alone.

'From Gien we went to Fierbois and I was able to attend Mass at the church and to worship at the foot of the statue of St Catherine. I was able to hear Mass three times in one day.'

'It's at Fierbois that you dictated a letter to the Dauphin telling him that you were on your way to help him and that you would be able to recognise him among many others.'

'Yes, I did. And it was probably that letter that tempted the Dauphin to play a trick on me when I went to see him.'

'Well then, let's go to Chinon now.'

# SECTION 3: CHINON

# Chapter 11: Tricks and Traps

Chinon is on the River Vienne in the Loire Valley about twelve kilometers from where the Vienne flows into the Loire. The castle was one of the strongest in France Even today the ancient towers and walls high on a ridge above the town are spectacular and seem to promise security and solidity. But it's an illusion quickly shattered. Inside all is in ruins.

It was once the home of the English King Henry II and Eleanor of Aquitaine.

In the time of Joan of Arc, Charles VII had set up his court here and no doubt the strong fortress gave him a sense of security. The walls rise out of the cliffs on every side of the chateau with a sheer drop to the town below. The chateau was actually three castles in one, a city within a city.

I arrived in Chinon by train from Paris and took a short walk to the hotel I had booked at number 10, Place Jeanne d'Arc, *The Golden Lion*. I left my bag in my room and headed out again.

I checked out the sculpture of Joan on horseback in full charge, sword held high in one hand, banner in the other. Her horse is leaping over the body of a fallen soldier. Joan is leaning back in the saddle like one of the screaming Valkyries. The stone pedestal holds her so high, I could imagine the horse sailing right over me and careering down the street with Wagnerian music accompanying it. Joan loved to ride and her excellent horsemanship is still a puzzle. I think she would have liked this statue by Jules Rolleau.

I made my way up to the chateau, paid my entrance money and looked around. All that remains of the Grand Hall where Joan finally met her Dauphin are a wall and a fireplace.

Joan joined me and looked around at the ruins. We sat down on a small part of a wall and, without any prompting, she continued her story.

'We rode to Chinon from Fierbois leaving at dawn and arriving about noon. It was March 6. I remember it was Lent because I had been fasting.'

I interrupted her. 'That wasn't necessary for a seventeen-year-old was it?'

'No but I chose to do it. Anyway, I found lodging not far from the castle in an inn with a respectable woman running it. Then I sent another message to the Dauphin to let him know I had arrived.

'Charles sent his Council members to interview me. At first I refused to talk to them as I wanted to speak only to the Dauphin.

'They argued with me, insisting, "But we have been sent by the Dauphin; we come in his name".

'Finally I agreed to speak to them.

'I told them, "The King of Heaven has sent me to raise the siege of Orléans and to have the Dauphin crowned King of France in the cathedral of Reims."

'They looked at me and then at each other in amazement. One of them cleared his throat and said, "We will consider what you have said and advise the Dauphin of our verdict."

'They filed out of the room muttering to each other and some of them looked back at me as if I were some sort of talking dog – a female talking dog at that.

'They obviously couldn't reach a unanimous decision. They reported to the Dauphin with a divided verdict. Some told him he should see me but some of those closest to him advised him against it.'

I asked, 'Why would they do that? What harm could there be in your seeing and speaking with the Dauphin so he could make his own mind up?'

'Exactly. As I spent more time at court, I began to understand some of the politics of it. There were four men in particular who opposed me and I understood later that they feared I might gain more influence over the Dauphin than they had.'

'Who were they?'

'The most influential was La Trémoille. You couldn't miss him. He was so fat. I think he hated me from the start. He was Charles's favourite at the time. Charles was always out of money and Trémoille had lent him a great deal over a period of time so, apart from dominating him personally, he also had a financial hold over him.'

'How did you get to see the Dauphin in spite of this opposition?'

'The Dauphin was still curious about me so he asked some of the churchmen to interview me. They came to see me and I told them much the same thing I had told the Council. They apparently believed me because they advised the Dauphin to see me.

'Meanwhile, my companions De Metz and Poulengy had been telling everyone who would listen about our journey from Vaucouleurs, about rivers marvelously forded and dangers marvelously escaped. Charles even interviewed them himself. But he still wouldn't interview me.

'After two days of indecision, he finally sent for me. The great hall of the Royal Lodging inside the fortress was prepared and the court assembled there. I estimate there were some three hundred knights and various other people waiting to have a look at me.

'It was evening and I walked up the steep hill to the main drawbridge under the clock tower to go in to the castle.'

Again I interrupted. 'Isn't this where you predicted a man's death and it happened?'

'That's true,' she replied. 'As I reached the drawbridge, a man on horseback pulled up and stared at me. He shouted out to anyone who would listen. "*Jarnidieu!* Isn't that the virgin? If I could have her for one night, I wouldn't return her in the same condition."

'*Jarnidieu* was a French swear word of the time and it meant "I deny God".

'So I said to him, "In God's name, you deny Him and you so near your death."

'I continued on into the castle. The story goes that he fell into the river and drowned an hour later.'

'That was pretty amazing. How did you know?'

Again Joan shrugged. 'I don't know. I would get a sense of these things and trust that they were true.'

I had to be content with that so I changed tack. 'At last you were going to meet the Dauphin. You mentioned he played a trick on you. Tell me about that.'

'As you know, I had sent a letter to him from Fierbois and in it I had written that I would recognise him among many others. He arranged to hide himself among the members of the court.

'When I arrived, Louis of Bourbon, a royal prince, came out to meet me and took me by the hand. He treated me like a lady of equal rank to himself and led me into the hall. It was packed with people and there were about fifty torches lighting up the place. I remember it was hot and smoky.'

'Did you dress up for the occasion?' I asked as I contemplated Joan among all the brightly dressed courtiers.

'I was wearing the clothes I had traveled in, the outfit bought for me at Vaucouleurs by de Metz and Poulengy. It was a black doublet with leggings, a grey tunic over that, black boots and a black hat.'

'So you were still dressed as a boy?'

'Yes. It must have looked quite a sight with the prince solemnly leading the page boy by the hand. He took me up to one of the men and introduced him as the king. I immediately knew it was not the king and said so. Then another man presented himself to me as the king but again I knew it wasn't the king.'

I thought of the portrait of Charles that I had seen in the Louvre. It had been painted by Jean Fouquet in Charles' lifetime. The droopy eyelids and bulbous nose were very distinctive but Joan would not have seen a painting of him.

She continued, 'I looked around and spotted him partly hiding behind some of his courtiers. I walked over to him and took off my hat. "God give you good life, gentle king."

'Even then he continued testing me. "Joan," he said, "It is not I who is king," and he pointed to yet another courtier.

'I stood my ground and replied to him "In God's name, gentle prince. It is you and none other."

'Finally, he smiled and I said "Very noble Lord Dauphin, I am come and am sent by God to bring help to you and your kingdom."

'With this, he took me by the arm and led me apart from the rest of the crowd so no one could hear our words. It was then that I spoke with him about something that only he knew. I have not revealed that to anyone although there has been a lot written about it.'

'Yes,' I broke in. 'It's been assumed that you said something to calm his doubts about his legitimacy to the throne. Is that right?'

Joan smiled. 'Yes, I said that to him but that is no secret. It was later in private in his room where he interviewed me further, that I told him something else that convinced him I was genuine. There was a story which surfaced almost a hundred years later that I had revealed the contents of his secret prayers on one occasion and this convinced him to trust me. But, since I swore to tell no one, pass on to the next question.'

I smiled at the phrase. 'Pass on. That's what you used to say to the judges at your trial when you didn't intend to answer. But at your trial, you did tell the judges what the sign was that you gave the king. You made up a story about an angel with a crown and later admitted you had made the whole thing up. What was that about?'

Joan looked distressed and there were tears in her eyes. For a moment I wished I hadn't asked the question.

'There are things I said and did in those last few days of my life that I am deeply ashamed of. I make no excuses for them but perhaps we could talk about them when we come to discussing the trial.'

'All right;' I agreed. 'Please don't cry. Let's pass on.

# Chapter 12: My Bonny Duke

Joan composed her face and wiped her tears with the back of her hand

'You had recognised the Dauphin and had a private conversation with him. So what happened next?'

Joan thought a moment and a happy smile lit up her whole face.

'It was at Chinon that I met *mon beau duc*, Jean, Duke of Alençon. He had been away shooting quail when he heard that his cousin the Dauphin was interviewing a seventeen year-old girl who claimed to be sent by God to raise the siege of Orléans. His curiosity was so high that he returned to Chinon the next day to see for himself. I was with the Dauphin in his private apartment when the prince arrived.

'As he walked in, I asked Charles, "Who is this?"

'He replied, "This is my cousin, Jean, Duke of Alençon." Then turning to Alençon, he said, "Welcome cousin, welcome."

'I turned to Alençon and greeted him warmly. "You are very welcome," I said. "The more we have of the royal blood of France the better."

'We liked each other immediately.'

*Jean, Duke of Alençon*

Joan looked wistful as the memories of her *beau duc* came flooding back. He was twenty years of age when they met. These two young people were to experience so much together of triumph and tragedy as comrades-in-arms and friends but that story lay ahead of us. I waited till she was ready to continue.

'I saw him again the next day when we heard Mass with the Dauphin. After Mass, Charles sent everyone away except La Trémoille who was almost always with him, the Duke of Alençon and myself. We talked for a couple of hours and I made the point several times that Charles must give the Kingdom of France over to God and God would give it back to him. We then went in to dinner and, after dinner, the Dauphin went off by himself into the meadows nearby. I also went out with a lance and practised tilting. I did not realise Alençon was watching me. Apparently he admired my skill and later gave me a horse as a gift.'

I asked another question. 'Before you left Domremy you had not learnt to ride a horse and the trip from Vaucouleurs to Chinon by horseback had left you with a very sore behind. Yet in the days and months that followed, many people commented on your skill as a horsewoman. How did you become so good so quick-ly?'

'I think it was partly because I was strong and fit. That allowed me to use my muscles in harmony with the horse. Also I believed that I could do anything I needed to do to accomplish my mission. Belief can be a powerful force and it removes fear. It's fear that causes tension and lack of co-ordination. Horses can sense fear in a rider so it was an advantage that I did not feel fear of them.'

I had to agree it sounded plausible. 'Did you spend any more time with the Duke?'

'Yes. A few days later he took me to St Florent to stay with his wife and his mother for three or four days. His wife, also called Jeanne, greeted me very warmly and we had several long conversations. They were married when they were both fourteen years of age and he had been captured by the English in 1424, only a year after they were married. He had only just been released after five years in prison. The ransom she had paid for him had cost them a great deal. All she wanted now was for him to stay home quietly with her. I felt very sad for her situation but I knew Jean would not take to domestic life when there were English to fight.

'I said to her, "Madame, fear nothing. I will bring him back to you as safe and well as he is now, or even better."'

'In fact you saved his life at one stage, didn't you?'

'That's true,' she said.

'So did Charles send you off to relieve the siege of Orléans?'

'No. Weeks went by. Charles still wanted more tests and examinations done on me. Madame de Trèves and Madame de Gaucourt were even asked to examine me to see if I was a boy or a girl. Still, I was treated well and I was moved into my own rooms in the Tower of Coudray, within the castle. I had my own chapel attached to my room so that I could pray there whenever I wanted to. I was given a page boy, [5]Louis de Coutes. He was fourteen years old and was with me all the time except at night when women were sent to stay with me. I was able to see and speak with the Dauphin at any time I wanted to.'

'How did you get on with the other members of the court?'

'Most of them probably thought I was an entertaining diversion in an otherwise predictable circle of events and intrigues. As I said before, those who liked to think they had some influence over Charles, saw me as quite a threat. Anyway, the Dauphin sent men of high standing to interview me and give their opinion of me. Then he

---

[5] In earlier translations, Louis de Coutes was mistakenly recorded as Contes.

decided to send me off to be examined by the most important churchmen around. I didn't know where we were going but it turned out to be Poitiers. I was aware that it wasn't going to be an easy examination but I trusted in God's help. Let's meet in Poitiers and I'll tell you what happened next.'

# SECTION 4: POITIERS

# Chapter 13: Put to the Test

Poitiers today is a country town set on a hilltop overlooking two rivers. This was the home of that other great woman, Eleanor of Aquitaine who had lived here almost three hundred years before Joan's arrival. Eleanor's ancestral home still stands and serves as the Palace of Justice.

I met Joan in the amazing Church of Notre Dame. It seems every second church in France is called Notre Dame but this one was definitely unique. It was difficult to take my eyes off the patterned and brightly coloured columns and the very human sculptures. We seated ourselves on one side of the church and Joan began to speak without waiting for questions.

'I was happy here. It seemed I was getting closer to my goal of helping the people in Orléans but, I must admit, I came close to losing my temper a few times.'

'When was that?' I asked.

'During the examination. There was one of the examiners questioning me. Brother Seguin was his name. He was no fool, I'll grant him that. He was a Carmelite monk and became Professor of Theology at the University of Poitiers when it was founded a year or so later. He was a Frenchman from Limousin I think. He spoke French like someone from Yorkshire might speak English.

'At one stage, he asked me in what language my voices spoke to me.

I replied "A better language than yours."

'The whole assembly laughed. I only meant to tease him and I think he knew that. But he went on and on. He said they could not advise the Dauphin to trust me until I gave them some proof. I admit I snapped a little.

"In God's name" I said, "I have not come to Poitiers to perform signs. Lead me to Orléans, and I will show you the signs for which I am sent."

'I then let them know my agenda. I told them that once I was put at the head of the army, Orléans would be freed, the English would be destroyed, the Dauphin would be crowned at Reims, Paris would again give its allegiance to Charles, and the Duke of Orléans would be returned from imprisonment in England.'

'How did they react?'

Joan laughed. 'I could see they were more than a bit stunned at my cheek. Those were pretty amazing claims to be making.'

I agreed. 'Yes but although those things happened as you predicted only two of them occurred before your death.'

Joan looked sad. Finally, she spoke: 'At that stage I didn't know I was going to die so soon. The voices did tell me I had only one year to accomplish my mission but they didn't mention that I was going to die and they certainly didn't mention how I was going to die. I had just turned seventeen. I was full of life, I believed in what I was doing, God was on my side. I had the excitement of my mission and most seventeen year-olds think they're immortal anyway.'

'That certainly hasn't changed,' I said. 'What happened next at the examination?'

'As I said, they were all a bit stunned by what I was claiming but one of them, Guillaume Aymerie, thought he'd catch me out.

'He said: "You say your voices tell you that God wishes to free the people of France from their present calamities. But if He wishes to free them, it is not necessary to have an army."

'I snapped back at him: "In God's name, the men-at-arms will fight and God will give them the victory."'

'Sort of God helps-those-who-help-themselves!' I laughed. 'You were very confident and even quite cheeky in front of all those high-ranking churchmen. Amazing for a seventeen-year old girl from a farm in the backblocks.'

'Yes, I guess I was. But I trusted in God and my voices. Anyway, they finally decided, as Brother Seguin put it "… that, in view of the imminent necessity and of the danger of Orléans, the King might allow the girl to help him and might send her to Orléans."

'You put a lot of faith in the report of this examination and asked again and again for it to be sent for during your trial of condemnation in Rouen. Of course, it was not produced. Very embarrassing it would have been to have a report by churchmen endorsing you as worthy of trust and a messenger of God, when all that court in Rouen wanted to do was condemn you for the very opposite. It also appears that the Poitiers report disappeared even while you were still alive. It's never been found.'

'That's true but let's move on. All I wanted to do was get on with relieving the siege at Orléans and getting Charles crowned. But no – there were more delays. As I said before, I was sent to Tours for yet another physical examination to see if I were a boy or a girl and, if a girl, a virgin. Charles' mother-in-law, the Queen of Sicily was put in charge of this examination, with other ladies assigned to help. Once again, they reported that I was still a virgin.

'Was this embarrassing for you, Joan?'

'I certainly didn't like it but because of its importance to the beliefs of the time, I knew I just had to put up with it. So I did. I was examined so many times, I was getting used to it by the end.'

'So now the way was clear for you to get on with your mission?'

'Yes. I was given what was called a "regular household", a number of men whose task was to look after me in various ways. I was given two pages, Louis de Coutes as I told you earlier and another boy, Raymond, my standard bearer. Jean d'Aulon was appointed my squire by the Dauphin.'

I interrupted. 'The Bastard of Orléans called Jean d'Aulon the most honest man in the French army, in his testimony at your rehabilitation trial.'

'Yes, he was a brave and loyal soldier and companion. He fought under the command of the Bastard in 1427. In the battle to raise the siege of Montargis, he had four horses killed under him.' She paused as if remembering her friend, then went on. 'I was also given two heralds, two servants and my own confessor, Jean Paqueral. To me, at the time, this was the best of all. Now I could hear Mass and have my confession heard whenever I wanted. I often did this more than once a day.'

'You were deeply religious, obviously, and loved the rituals of the Church.'

'Yes, I was. It sustained me through so much. Just one more thing about my retinue – my brother, Pierre, came from Domremy to join me. Brother Jean came later.'

I continued. 'It was while you were at Poitiers that you wrote an extremely provocative letter to the English. You dictated it to your examiners and they wrote it down for you.'

'Yes – as I told you, I never learnt to read or write.'

'You addressed it to the King of England, and the English leaders in France, as well as those soldiers besieging Orléans, telling them to surrender all the towns and wealth they had captured in France, and to go back to England. If they did this, the French would show them mercy and let them go. If they didn't, they would be soundly defeated. You claimed in the letter that you were sent by God, the King of Heaven.'

'Yes. They did not believe me and a lot of people died unnecessarily.' She looked so sad that I continued speaking to give her time to compose herself.

'By this point,' I said, 'many people's attitude had totally changed. News of your mission had preceded you even before you saw the Dauphin and from then on you were seen as the saviour of France. Soldiers, townspeople, even aristocracy, adored you. People tried to kiss your hands and feet.'

'Yes – it was all amazing and a bit embarrassing but it was quite a change from being that crazy girl from Domremy to Joan the Maid, the hope of France. Even before I had actually accomplished anything! I was given armour and a banner and a sword. I refused the sword as I had one in mind already.'

# Chapter 14: I had a Banner

'Finding your sword,' I said. 'This is one of the many amazing parts of your story. You said a sword for you would be found buried in the ground behind the church of Saint Catherine at Fierbois. You sent a letter to the priests of St Catherine asking them to find the sword for you. Sure enough, when they looked where you had said, the sword was found. It was very rusty but when they started to clean it, the rust fell off easily. It was engraved with five crosses. How did you know it was there? Not even the people in Fierbois knew it was there.'

'My voices told me about it. Next question.'

'In paintings and statues of you, you're usually shown holding a banner. Tell me about that.'

'I had a banner with the background covered with lilies. The world was painted on it, with two angels at the sides; it was a white cloth called boucassin; on it was written *Jhesus Maria* and it was fringed with silk.

'Actually, there were two banners, the large standard and a smaller pennon, both made by a painter we called Hauves Poulnoir. His real name was Hamish Power, a Scotsman living in France. He was paid 25 livres-tournois [6]for his service, and I also tried to help

---

[6] The *livre-tournois* was the standard of currency used in France at the time. *Livre* is the French word for pound. The original *livre* was established by Charlemagne as a unit of accounting having the value of one pound of silver. Different regions gradually produced currency of different values. The area ruled by the Kings of France used the *livre Parisis* (the

his daughter Héliote during her wedding by asking the officials of Tours to provide her dowry.

'The small pennon had an Annunciation scene with an angel presenting a lily to the Virgin Mary, on a white background.

I smiled and continued. 'At your trial of condemnation, they asked again and again various questions about your banner. They asked which did you love most, your banner or your sword.'

Joan nodded. 'I told them I loved my sword because it was found in the church of St Catherine. When they asked me about the sword or the banner, I replied that I loved the banner forty times better.'

'What did you tell them when they asked why you carried your banner into battle?'

'I told them the truth. I didn't want to use my sword. It was in order to avoid killing anybody with my own hands. I never killed anyone. Let's go to Orléans. I'll meet you there.'

---

Paris Pound). When the independent county of Anjou was overtaken by the French King, the currency of Anjou, the *livre tournois* (the Tours pound) was adopted as the standard within France, gradually replacing the *livre parisis*.

# SECTION 5: ORLÉANS

# Chapter 15: The City of Orléans

'I'll meet you in Orléans,' she had said. I returned from Poitiers to my Paris hotel in the Rue des Artes and a day later, I took the hour and a half train journey to Orléans, the town which was the scene of Joan's first great military triumph. She is often called The Maid of Orléans because she raised the seven-month long siege of the city, defeating the English for the first time in decades. The title "Maid of Orléans" wasn't applied to her in her lifetime though. That was added later as her legend grew.

From the station, I walked out into Place d'Arc, and across to yet another statue of Joan on horseback carrying a sword. Quite different from the dynamic statue in Chinon. Here Joan sits quietly in the saddle holding out her sword as if offering it to someone. It's a beautiful statue with bas relief panels depicting the highlights of her short life. There, on a long panel on one side of the pedestal, is Joan leading the relief of Orléans. It's a scene of death, determination and chaos and Joan is right in the thick of it.

I walked around the pedestal, stopping at each side to look at the detailed sculpting. There is Joan being pulled from her horse at her capture outside Compiègne. Next is Joan in her prison cell, chained to a block of wood. The English guards are amusing themselves by jeering and laughing at her and pulling on the chain that is attached to her leg.

And finally, the scene of her death by fire. Agony, jeering soldiers and remorseful priests.

Sadly, some of the key figures in the scenes have been vandalized.

A short walk from the square took me to the house of Joan of Arc, a three-storey plastered building with an attic. The windows are made of small panes of glass and surrounded by white bricks. The windows on the ground floor were covered by solid wooden shutters and the door was bolted. Like everything else to do with Joan, the house was closed between 12 noon and 2 p.m. so I went looking for somewhere to have lunch and wait.

I found a quiet seat in La Brasserie, a café in rue de Gourville, and settled down. I chose from the menu and ordered a meal with a *pichon* of wine. When the wine arrived, I took a sip and looked around.

The large black and white tiles on the floor of the restaurant reminded me of a huge chess board and I thought of Joan, both knight and pawn in a game of political, religious and gender politics. Lunch arrived and I found myself enjoying it immensely in spite of my thoughts. I poured another glass of wine and wrote a few letters home.

At two o'clock I entered Maison de Jeanne d'Arc. This is where Joan stayed after she entered Orléans in triumph on 29 April, 1429. The house belonged to Jacques Boucher who was treasurer to the Duke Charles d'Orléans. The original house was completely destroyed by bombs in World War 2 but the present house has been re-constructed using materials from other bombed houses of the same era.

Joan slept up on the first floor with a window overlooking the street below. The room contained a few replicas – a life-size model of Joan and a copy of her banner. It was warm and peaceful and I stood with eyes closed imagining Joan here with her page Louis and the townsfolk in the street below clamouring to see their young hero. It was here that Louis lent out the window and handed her banner down to Joan on her horse below before she sped off to fight the English.

I thought she might have joined me here but she did not. I walked back down the stairs and into the street.

Walking along the rue Jeanne d'Arc, I entered the Cathedral of Orléans. Again, a beautiful set of stained glass windows depicts her life.

Standing in the cathedral, I gazed from one exquisite window to the next and the scenes began to blur into a kaleidoscope of colours without form. The tears filled my eyes and ran down my cheeks. What use was all this to Joan? In the end, they burnt her.

I sat down at the back of the cathedral and waited for Joan to join me. I did not have long to wait.

There was a whisper beside me. 'Hello.'

She had joined me as promised. 'Hello Joan. Here we are in the town where your legend and fame really took off.'

'Yes – it was an exciting time.'

# Chapter 16: The Arrival

'When you left Poitiers, how did you get to Orléans and who went with you?'

'We left from Blois near Poitiers on 27 April. Jeanne de Metz and Poulengy were with me. You may remember they had first accompanied me from Vaucouleurs to Chinon when I was unknown. They were faithful friends and comrades-at-arms. My brothers, Pierre and Jean, also came with me. Funny that. Remember how Father had told them to drown me if I ever went off with soldiers? Nice twist, don't you think. There they were, soldiers with me.

'There were also some very well known captains with me. Saint Sévère, de Rais, Louis de Culen, Ambroise de Loré and La Hire. They're all just names now – except for de Rais. He became quite famous later, or should I say infamous. He was the legendary Bluebeard although we knew none of that at the time. He was a brave and loyal soldier when he was with me.'

'Many people assume you were in command of the army but that's not quite true, is it?'

Joan laughed and looked down at her hands for a moment.

'It's true though that I did take matters into my own hands from time to time. I made them change their ways in the army. Got them to go to confession, stop swearing and got rid of all the women camp followers and prostitutes that accompanied the army. La Hire in particular was well known for his violent swearing and

I made him stop. I did let him use my own two expressions though.'

'You swore? What two expressions were they?'

Joan laughed. 'Yes. I had a couple of expressions I'd use when I was excited or angry or frustrated or all of the above. They were *en nom Dieu* and *par mon martin*. They mean "In God's name" and "By my staff". Fairly innocuous.'

I nodded and returned to the issue of command. 'So although you were not officially in charge, they obeyed you?'

'Yes, they did. And more so after what happened at Orléans.'

'It was remarkable, Joan. You were about eighteen years old by then and female.'

'Yes, that's right. I was the only woman among those thousands of men. They followed me and, for the most part, they obeyed me. On the way to Orléans, we slept in the fields and I did not remove my armour. I was conscious of sleeping among the men and considered it sensible to remain fully dressed. It was very uncomfortable and I was tired and bruised in the morning but it was worth it.'

Again that practical recognition of the reality of a woman alone among many men and the need to minimize her attraction and provide protection by wearing male clothes.

'We continued on towards Orléans. It rained all day and was thoroughly miserable. Talk about drowned rats. That's just how we felt and tempers were not the best. The next evening we camped just one mile south of Orléans on the bank of the river Loire. I was furious!'

'Why? They had finally brought you to Orléans, hadn't they?'

'Yes, but on the wrong side of the river!'

'What do you mean? Didn't all these great captains know what they were doing?'

'Oh, they knew what they were doing all right. I was so angry because I believed they had tricked me. You'll have to look at the map to see what I mean. Here let me draw you another map.'

I handed her my notebook and pen. She studied the tip of the ballpoint pen for a moment, made a few tentative strokes on the paper then drew her map as she talked.

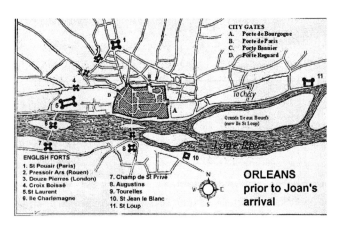

'The Loire River runs along the south side of Orléans and it's about 400 metres wide at that point. There was a stone bridge of nineteen arches across the river leading to the southern gateway into the city. It was called Porte du Pont (Bridge Gate). You can see on the map, at the southern end of the bridge there was a two-towered fortress gatehouse, called 'Les Tourelles' (number 8 on the map). A drawbridge connected Les Tourelles to another fortification called a barbican (number 9), on the river's southern bank. This barbican was an enclosed compound, with earthwork, wood timber, and part masonry walls. I'm telling you this because it is important later in the story.'

I nodded and said, 'So there you were on the south side of the river. Why was that a problem?'

'I had expected we would go round to the west and the north of the city, skirting behind the enemy and entering by the eastern gate. That was the one side of the city that was poorly guarded by the English and we could still get men and supplies in by that gate.

'Instead of that, they had brought me straight to Orléans. They intended to ferry the supplies and cattle we had brought across the river, further upstream at a place called Chécy, then ride back to Orléans from there. Here I was in sight of the place I had spent so long persuading people, including the Dauphin, to take me to, and these captains intended me to ride docilely upstream to Chécy and cross in a boat, then come back to Orléans. I guess my disappointment got the better of me and I tore strips off everyone in sight.'

'Not a good introduction to the Bastard of Orléans from what I've read.'

Again, Joan laughed.

'You're so right. The poor Bastard came across from the town in a boat to meet and welcome me to his city. It was pouring with rain. He got out of the boat and came towards me. He was dripping wet as he strode up the muddy bank. I didn't wait for him to speak. I let him have it.

'I said, "Is it you who are the Bastard of Orléans?"

'He remained gracious, I have to say.

'He replied "I am and I rejoice in your arrival."

'Not good enough for me so I shouted back at him:

"Is it you who advised them to bring me here by the bank of this river, instead of sending me straight to Talbot and his English?"

"Others wiser than I also thought it best for your safety as well as that of the supplies you bring."

'I was getting angrier with every word and I almost screamed at him.

"*En nom Dieu*! The counsel of our Lord is better and wiser than yours. You thought to deceive me, but you have deceived yourselves, for I bring you the finest help that ever was brought to knight or to city, since it is the help of the King of Heaven!"

I laughed. 'He probably thought he was going to meet a gentle saintly girl not a screaming woman in armour.'

'True, I admit I was pretty full on. We became good friends after that but it was a rocky start.'

'Before you go on, tell me about the term "bastard". In our time it's not very polite to call someone a bastard although if the tone of voice is right, it can sometimes be a term of affection.'

'Although his real name was John of Dunois, he preferred to be called the Bastard of Orléans because at that time it was a term of respect. It acknowledged and highlighted the fact that he was of noble blood, half brother to the Duke of Orléans and cousin to the King.

The Duke of Orléans was a prisoner of war in England at the time and the Bastard was acting head of the Dukedom in his absence.'

'I see. So what happened next – on the wrong side of the river?'

'As I said, they intended to bring boats out of the city and sail them up-river to Chécy where they would cross and ferry the cattle, the supplies and myself across the river and then ride the five miles back to the east gate of Orléans. The Bastard had no intention of taking on the English until he got the food safely into his city. Looking back on it now, I can see the wisdom of it. Their whole plan came unstuck though because the wind was blowing the wrong way. They couldn't sail the boats up to Chécy! So, with nothing else to do, I simply told them all to wait a little and all would be well. And then the wind changed.'

# Chapter 17: The Welcome and the Not-so-Welcome

And then the wind changed! I smiled at the simplicity of the statement. 'A miracle.'

'Well it certainly seemed like it to everyone. But I still had problems with the Bastard. He considered the army I had brought with me was not large enough to take on the English. It had been good enough to escort the much-needed supplies to Orléans but now, the Bastard wanted them to go back to Blois and leave me with him. The townspeople of Orléans apparently had heard much of me and were eager to see me.

'I did not want to leave my army. They had loyally obeyed me in all that I had demanded of them. My captains did not want to part with me either and it looked as though we would all head back to Blois and leave the Bastard to his own devices. He managed to persuade the captains to return to Blois and get more troops, then return by the north to enter the city in the way I had originally thought they should. They in turn promised me that they would return soon. So I stayed.

'We crossed the river and I spent the night in Ché-cy, so near to my goal of Orléans but not quite there.' Joan paused and we both looked at the map she had drawn.

To be honest, reading about the siege, I thought the English were pretty sloppy in their attitude and actions. They didn't totally surround the town and some supplies could still be brought in through the eastern gate of the town which the English don't seem to have bothered about. They built towers and defence works on the other three sides but left the eastern side almost undefended.

We needed some background so I asked, 'Why was Orléans an important step in your story and why did the English bother to besiege it in the first place?'

Joan took up the story. 'Their best commander, Thomas Montacute, the Earl of Salisbury had fought many battles against the French in this long, long war. He returned to France in July 1428 with orders to lay siege to Angers. From Paris he took Rambouillet, Nogent-le-Roi and other places. Then he changed the plan of the campaign and decided, against the will of Bedford, the Regent of England, to undertake the siege of Orléans.

'He began the Siege of Orleans on the 12th October and, on the 23rd, his army drove the French out of their position defending Tourelles, the fortification I told you about at the southern end of the bridge into Orléans. On 24th October, he stormed Tourelles and ordered Sir William Glasdale to fortify and occupy it. While he was surveying the city from a window of Tourelles on 27th, a stone ball from a cannon shattered the stone and iron work of the window. The scattered shards hit the Earl full in the face. One of his eyes was destroyed and most of his face torn apart. He was carried to Meung and died there a week later. As he lay dying, he told the English captains never to give up the siege.

'His placement was the Earl of Suffolk who put Glasdale in charge of the Tourelles.

'How many people were involved?'

'It was a pretty even fight. Orléans had a population of about thirty thousand – about five thousand men capable of defending the town. I arrived with about three thousand men and around five or six thousand more arrived a few days later making a total of about ten or eleven thousand on the French side. The English had about ten or eleven thousand troops as well.'

'When did you finally get into Orléans?'

'Not till the next day or I should say evening. It was Friday, 29th April. The people of Orléans had become so excited at the news of my arrival that it was decided to hold off entering the town until the evening to avoid a crush of people. I was given a beautiful white horse for the occasion. I put on full armour and carried my white banner.

'We rode from Chécy to Orléans. The Bastard was riding on my left and he looked very grand in his armour and cloak and a magnificent horse. My brothers, Pierre and Jean were with me and so were my squire Jean d'Aulon and my page Louis. Behind them came many captains, soldiers and citizens. It was quite a parade. Even though we rode into the town in the semi-darkness, the crowds of people almost crushed us. They were shouting and trying to touch me and my horse. So many of them carried flaming torches because of the darkness, and one of the citizens came so close to me that his torch set light to my pennant. It was quickly extinguished so we rode on and ....'

I interrupted. 'People who saw your reaction to your pennant on fire were filled with admiration. It seems, you spurred your horse forward, turned him suddenly and put out the flames in one swirling movement. And you had never ridden a horse before going to see Robert de Baudricourt only a few months earlier.'

Joan looked surprised and laughed a little in embarrassment.

'Instinct, I guess. I enjoyed riding once I got the hang of it. Anyway, we continued right across the town from east to west. People were so happy. it was inspiring and very touching to see their faith. You would have thought the siege was already over. They took me to the home of Jacques Boucher. He was Treasurer to the Duke of Orléans. As soon as we arrived, I got Louis to help me take off my armour. I had been wearing it all day and had not eaten or drunk anything all day either. Supper was prepared for me but I just asked for half a glass of wine. I filled it with water and soaked some bread in it. That was all I wanted. And that night I slept very well.

'Next day, I went to see the Bastard. He didn't want to do anything. He wanted to wait till re-enforcements arrived from Blois. He figured that a four-day wait was worth it. Looking back on it now I feel sorry for him. He had me to put up with and I wasn't easy to get on with; he had the responsibility of defending his town in the way he saw best; he had hotheads like La Hire and Florent d'Illiers who wanted to attack the English immediately and he had other captains who just plain didn't want anything to do with a girl interfering in the battle plans.'

'He seems to have handled all of you with diplomacy and tact.'

Joan smiled and the affection on her face was plain. 'Yes, he was one of the best. You should have seen this one captain who gave him (and me) a hard time. The Sieur de Gamaches took exception to my role in affairs.

'He said to the Bastard "Since you pay more heed to the advice of a little saucebox of low birth than to a knight such as myself, I will no longer protest; when the time and the place come my good sword will speak; I may meet my end in the doing, but the King and my honour demand it. Henceforth I lower my banner and am no more than a simple squire. I prefer to have a noble man as my master than a hussy who may once have been God knows what."

'He furled his banner and handed it to the Bastard.'

'That was a pretty dramatic little tantrum!' I commented.

'Yes but the Bastard and the other captains persuaded Gamaches and me to kiss on the cheek and make up. Neither of us wanted to but we did in the end.'

'Did you feel frustrated that you weren't going to be attacking the English that day?'

'No, I wanted to give them the opportunity to move out and return to England without bloodshed. Remember, when I was in Poitiers, I wrote a letter to have delivered to the commanders at Orléans. People say it was a very arrogant letter but I fully believed that my mission was from God and when you're serving the one at the top, there's plenty of room for confidence. I wrote that they should get out of France and if they did not I would have them all put to death. I told them they should obey me because I was sent by the King of Heaven. And a whole lot more along those lines.

'The letter was carried with me and, on that first day in Orléans, I sent my two heralds, Ambleville and Guienne to deliver it to the English commander, Talbot. What a barbarian that man was. Heralds were conventionally treated neutrally so that communication could be carried out but he put poor Guienne in irons and had a stake set up ready to burn him. Even then the English had begun to believe I was a witch and they were going to burn Guienne in my place. Talbot sent Ambleville back to me with a very insulting message and many rude words telling me to go home and mind the cows or they would catch me and burn me.

'I sent Ambleville straight back to Talbot. Poor Ambleville was terrified but I assured him he'd be all right. I told him to tell Talbot that if he armed himself, I would arm myself too and if he came out in front of the city, I would be there and if he captured me, he could burn me. But, I said, if I beat him then he should leave with his army and go back to his own country.

'Meanwhile, the Bastard, responded to the threats in his own way. He arrested the English heralds that were already in Orléans organising the exchange of prisoners. He threatened to kill the heralds and the English prisoners if Guienne or Ambleville were harmed.

'But even the English knew that burning a herald wasn't exactly good protocol so they sent to the University of Paris to get authorization to do it. Let's take a little break and I'll tell you the rest later.'

'But what happened to Guienne?' I said.

Joan smiled impishly. 'All in good time. We'll get to it.' And then she was gone.

# Chapter 18: Surrender to a Woman! Never!

Joan had left me quite abruptly, so I explored the town of Orléans further, found a quiet place for a coffee and waited. Before too long, Joan joined me.

'Sorry to rush off like that,' she said without greetings. 'I love this place and just wanted to have a look around. People were so good to me here.'

Eager to get on with the interview, I launched straight into the questions: 'So, apart from poor Guienne's predicament, and the insults the English hurled at you, the first day here in Orléans was pretty quiet.'

'No, not exactly. While I was privately talking to the Bastard, La Hire and Florent d'Illiers took matters into their own hands. They stirred up a few of the other officers and some of the townspeople and went out to attack the English on the north west side of the town. The English retreated into their fort (Saint Pouair, the one the English called Paris). The townspeople gathered straw and wood to set the fort alight but the English started to chant their battle cry 'Hurrah! Hurrah!' This always seemed to spook the French and they retreated back into the town. Several were killed or wounded or taken prisoner on both sides. It was the sort of useless hassling that had been going on at the siege for the previous six or seven months and accomplished absolutely nothing.

'I didn't know about it till later. When I left the Bastard, I was furious that he wanted to do nothing. I went out to Les Tourelles.

'Standing on the bridge over the Loire, I shouted to the commander there, Sir William Glasdale, "In God's name, give yourself and your companions up. Save your lives."

'The English soldiers called out to me, "Cowgirl! We'll burn you when we catch you."

'One of the English captains, the Bastard of Granville, called back to me, ridiculing the idea that they would surrender to a woman and calling the French men "miscreant pimps".

'The first time the English called me whore, harlot, witch and so forth, I actually burst into tears. I was sad and hurt. This time I was very angry and I shouted at them that they were all liars and that Glasdale would die without being shriven. That means without having a priest give him his final confession and blessing.'

'Yes,' I said. 'That prediction added to your reputation when it came true. But in this instance, it seems extraordinary that the English let you stand in front of them and made no attempt to fire arrows or attack you in any way other than verbally.'

'Yes – I think they thought because I was a woman, I wasn't worthy of being considered a military opponent and therefore it didn't occur to them to shoot me. They'd happily burn me but not treat me as an equal, as a fellow soldier, no way.

'The next day – it was Sunday, 1 May - the Bastard and my squire, Jean d'Aulon set off to Blois with some soldiers to recruit more men. La Hire and I rode out with some extra troops to protect their departure if necessary. The English did absolutely nothing. Strange but that's what happened.

'When I returned to the house I was staying in, the townspeople almost broke down the door in their efforts to see me so I spent the day riding through the streets of Orléans to satisfy them. I could hardly manage to ride my horse through the press of the crowds.'

'Those who saw you that day reported their amazement at the way you did manage your horse. Some said you were like a young man-at-arms who had been doing it all his life.'

Joan said nothing for a while; she seemed deep in thought.

The whole process of medieval warfare seemed amazingly slapdash to me, and I said, 'The next two days were very quiet, weren't they? It is unbelievable that the English made no attempt to attack while Dunois was away getting re-inforcements.'

'I agree', Joan replied. 'Many people have since assumed it was because I had terrified them. I don't think that was the case. They were as rude and dismissive of me as ever. It is hard to say why they didn't attack. It had been a pattern they had adopted over the months before I arrived and the whole siege seems to have been rather half heartedly conducted after Salisbury's death. Sad that so many died though.

'On the morning of Monday 2nd May, I rode out and checked the English positions. Many of the townspeople followed me on foot but the English did nothing. No arrows, not even the insults this time.

'The next day, garrisons from other towns began to arrive in Orléans and there was news that the French army was on its way from Blois. Still the English did nothing.

'On Wednesday 4 May, I rode out very early in the morning with 500 men to meet the returning army. They were bringing the promised re-enforcements and supplies of food. I rode across open countryside and still the English made no attempt to attack. We met up with the army and accompanied them back to Orléans. It was good to have the Bastard and d'Aulon back. Jean d'Aulon and I had a quiet lunch in my host's house and, just as we finished eating, the Bastard arrived to tell me that the English commander Falstaff was on his way to join the siege with supplies and re-enforcements for the English.

'I said to him "Bastard, Bastard, tell me as soon as he arrives. If he gets here without me knowing it I promise I will have your head taken off'."

'He took it well and said he had no doubt that I would do it. He left then and assured me he would let me know as soon as he knew.'

# Chapter 19: First Victory

'D'Aulon and I were both very tired and we went upstairs to rest. He lay on a couch and I and my hostess lay on the bed and slept. I woke suddenly knowing that I must attack the English immediately. I was sure my angels had told me this but I didn't know if I was to attack the English in the forts or attack Falstaff who was bringing them supplies.

'I woke Jean immediately and he was groggy with sleep and took a while to comprehend what I was saying. My page Louis was nowhere in sight so I ran downstairs, found him and told him to fetch my horse.

'I admit I was very stirred up and I said to him "Bloody boy, why did you not tell me that French blood is being shed?"

'He had no idea what I was talking about. Then I ran back upstairs and Madame Boucher and her daughter and Jean helped me into my armour. I then raced back downstairs to find Louis sitting astride my horse. I told him to get down and bring me my banner which I had left upstairs. I mounted my horse and Louis handed me my banner from the upstairs window. Meanwhile Jean had put his armour on and sent for his horse. I galloped off and Jean followed on his horse. Louis raced after me on foot.'

'People who saw you said you were going so fast that your horse's hooves struck sparks from the cobble stones. What was going on?'

'It seems that while I was sleeping, the citizens of Orléans had got themselves stirred up. They were

excited at my presence already and the arrival of the
army and supplies had buoyed them up to overconfi-
dence. They had armed themselves and headed out to
attack the English fort of Saint-Loup. This was the most
isolated of the forts. It stood on the river Loire to the
east of Orléans. As I've already said, most of the English
forts were to the south, west and north west of the
town. You'll remember I was able to enter Orléans from
the east because it was the least defended by the
English. I rode from the western side of the town to the
eastern gate, the Burgundy Gate. It was here I met the
first of the French wounded being brought back into the
city. I could never see French blood without my hair
standing on end.

'The Bastard and the other captains had heard the
commotion and came galloping with their men towards
Saint-Loup. When I arrived at the fort, I planted my
standard in the ditch in front of the fort. There were
about one hundred and fifty Englishmen in the fort and
they asked me to take them for ransom. I refused and
told them I intended to take them in spite of themselves.
They put up a good resistance and the fight lasted about
three hours.

'This particular fort had been built around an
abandoned church and the English retreated into the
belfry. There were only about forty of them left by then
and they dressed themselves in monks' clothing which
they found in the church. Dressed as monks, they came
out and begged for their lives. My men were hot with
the fire of battle and victory and intended to massacre
the English but I stopped them. They were taken into
Orléans as prisoners.

'This was the first time in this long war that the French had captured anything from the English. As St Loup was the only fort on the eastern side of Orléans, we could now bring supplies and re-enforcements in by the eastern gate without fear of attack.'

# Chapter 20: True Grit

'When I got back into the town, I went straight to see my confessor, Paqueral. I was very distressed at the many English who had died without confession and blessing. I was in tears and Paqueral heard my confession. I told him to tell our soldiers that they must confess their sins and give thanks to God and, if they did not do this, I would leave them. I also ordered that all the prostitutes were to be expelled from the army's camp.'

'You also told Paqueral that the siege would be over and the English gone within the next five days, didn't you?'

'Yes, I did. I told him that, since the following day, 5 May, was the Feast of the Ascension of the Lord, I would make no war that day, out of respect for the Feast.

'Later in the day, I wrote one more letter to the English, and tied it to an arrow which an archer then shot over to the English. In the letter, I asked them once more to leave France and return to their homeland. I also commented that I would have sent the message in the normal way except that they still held the herald I had sent with my first letter. I asked them to return him to me and I would free the English prisoners we had taken at Saint-Loup. They laughed at me and called me harlot and whore.'

'They still didn't take you seriously but the next day, the fighting began in earnest, didn't it?'

'Yes. We decided to attack and take the English fort of St Jean-le-Blanc number 10 on the map). As you can see from the map, it was also an isolated fort but to get to it, we had to cross the river. There are a number of islands in the river at that point and we were able to cross to the Ile aux Toiles. We then needed to use boats to form a bridge to the southern bank of the river. We started about 9 a.m. I remember. That was quite late in those days. Particularly in summer.'

'Were there many English soldiers in that fort?'

'No, not many at all and when they saw us land on the Ile aux Toiles and start to cross to their side of the river, they abandoned the fort altogether and took shelter with their comrades in the fort of the Augustins, a much bigger and stronger fort. I can't say I blame them. We were quite a large force but we could only bring a small number of men off the island at a time, so we had some soldiers on the southern bank and some still on the island waiting to cross.

'At that point, it was decided by three of the captains that, since we were not strong enough to attack the Augustins, we should retreat and they gave the order to do so. The English saw the opportunity to attack those of us who had reached the southern bank and came pouring out of their fort. La Hire was with me and the two of us mounted our horses and, with lances couched, we charged straight at them.'

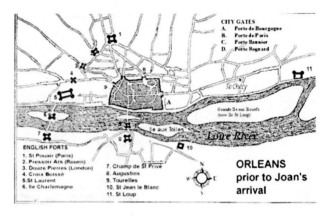

*This is the same map as that on page 58 reproduced here to make it easier to follow the story.*

'Just the two of you? It sounds like something out of a movie.'

Joan smiled at the modern reference. 'Initially yes, but when the rest of our soldiers saw what we were doing they turned around and, ignoring their captains' orders to retreat, came charging to help us.

'The men who were still on the Ile aux Toiles didn't wait for the boats; they leapt into the water up to their arm pits and waded ashore to join us. The English retreated to their fort Augustins but our soldiers were so inspired, they attacked the fort and entered it. I was one of the first to reach the fort and, jumping from my horse, I planted my standard at the base of the wall. It was at that point that I was wounded in the foot by a caltrop.'

'Oh, yes,' I said. 'I remember you mentioned them earlier. Nasty things. Same idea as our landmines today only not as deadly.'

'That's right,' she continued. 'Painful, debilitating but at least they didn't blow pieces off the body. They used to scatter them on the ground and they'd wound horses and foot soldiers.

'Our French soldiers stormed into the fort and killed most of the English. Some of the English managed to escape to the Tourelles. Our soldiers went berserk and began to loot the place. I was shocked at this lack of discipline and was also concerned that the much larger force of English troops from the Tourelles might decide to attack while our soldiers were intent on their looting. I ordered that the fort be set on fire and that forced them out of there.

'Many of our soldiers camped out that night to keep watch on the Tourelles. The town crier went through the town asking people to provide food and drink for the soldiers and citizens who remained outside. I intended to stay with them but the captains insisted I return inside the town. They knew I had been wounded and they could see I was exhausted.

# Chapter 21: You have been to your Council and I to Mine

'Usually, I fasted on Fridays but this day, when I returned to Boucher's house, I was happy to have some supper. While I was eating, the captains had a war council of their own and then one of them came to tell me they had decided not to attack the English the following day but to wait for re-enforcements. I was furious.

'I said to him: "You have been to your council and I to mine. And believe me, the counsel of my Lord will be put into effect, while your counsel will perish."

'What I didn't know was that they had also decided to guard the gates to prevent any of our soldiers from going out to attack the Tourelles. I found that out the hard way the next day.'

I interrupted. 'It was at this point that you repeated your prediction that you would be wounded, wasn't it?'

'Yes, I turned to Paqueral my priest who was standing beside me and said: "Get up early tomorrow, even earlier than you did today, and do your very best. Keep close to me at all times. For tomorrow the blood will spurt from my body above the breast."'

'You had predicted this event earlier too.'

'Yes. Long before I went to Orléans. I told the Dauphin that it would happen. But I also told him I would raise the siege and have him crowned in Reims so I knew I wasn't going to die from the wound.'

'He may have told someone else about it because we do know that it was recorded in a letter written in

Lyons on 22 April. A couple of weeks before it happened.'

'Unfortunately, knowing about it ahead of time didn't make it any easier to bear the pain. There was one other isolated English fort called Champ de St Privé (number 7 on the map). The English decided to abandon it rather than have it meet the same fate that St Loup and St Jean-le-Blanc had. They set it on fire and scrambled into boats to get across the river to safety in the main English camp at St Laurent. In their haste, at least one of the boats overturned and the men were pulled down by their armour and drowned. The citizens of Orléans were delighted to see the flames from the fort but we only found out about the drownings some time later.

'The next day, I got up very early and Paqueral sang Mass as I had requested him to do. I was about to leave the house when a deputation of citizens arrived. They were very angry at the captains' decision not to attack the English that day. The whole town had been in a state of excitement all night after the success at Augustins and there was no way they wanted to stop now.

'I mounted my horse and said to them: "In God's name I will do it and he who loves me will follow me."

'I was also worried about the soldiers and citizens who had stayed outside the city walls all night and wanted to make sure they were safe. I rode across the town to the Burgundy gate and quite a gathering of citizens and soldiers followed me. It was still dark when I arrived at the gate and it was then that I discovered it was guarded and that the captain, de Gaucourt, was not letting anyone out.

'Once again I was furious. Why couldn't these little men just let me get on with the job I had come to do! The crowd behind me were turning ugly and Gaucourt could see that he was in danger of being torn to pieces if he didn't let us through. He opened the gates and I rode through with the crowd following. We crossed the river and arrived at the Tourelles just as the sun was rising. Around 6 a.m. Quite a difference from the previous day's late start.

'The French outside the town had already begun preparations for storming the Tourelles. There were cannons and battering rams on the south side of the fort ready to attack. On the river side, materials had been gathered to build arches to get into the fort.

# Chapter 22: Wounded but Winning

'I called a council of war. This was the first one I had called. Previously, the captains had arranged to meet and then informed me later of their decisions. We planned to attack from the south side and scale the walls of the fort.

'At 7 a.m. the trumpets were sounded and the attack began. The English fought with great resistance. As fast as we put scaling ladders up to the walls, they attacked us with everything including cannon, firearms, axes, lances and even their bare hands. It was said at the time that there was so much "artificial fire" that the air seemed to be alight. But our soldiers seemed to think they were immortal and continued to attack in spite of the setbacks.

'We paused for a midday meal and then attacked again. I led the men back to the fort and was placing a scaling ladder against the wall when I was hit by a crossbow bolt. The arrow went into my neck and through my shoulder. I admit that even though I knew it was going to happen, I was afraid and I cried. Paqueral was there with me as I had asked him to be and he held me while I pulled the arrow out. A couple of soldiers saw what had happened and ran up, offering to put a charm on the wound. I told them I considered such things to be a sin, against God's law and I would rather die than use them. I asked for a cure that would not be a sin. They put olive oil and pig's grease on the wound and bound it with cotton to stop the bleeding.

'Our soldiers continued to attack until it was nearly evening but we were not making any headway. The Bastard decided there was no hope of victory that day and was going to call the retreat. I went up to him and asked him to wait just a little longer, to rest a little and to have something to eat. I then mounted my horse and rode in to a vineyard some distance away from the battle. I stayed there several minutes and prayed then I heard the trumpet sound the retreat. I could not believe it. I rushed back to the battle scene.

'It is here that your squire d'Aulon took matters into his own hands, wasn't it?'

'Yes. Bless him. He had no intention of retreating. I had earlier promised the men that when they saw the wind blowing my banner in the direction of the fort, then they would capture it. My banner was in the hands of a standard bearer who had taken it when I was wounded. The standard bearer had handed it over to a Basque soldier whom d'Aulon knew. D'Aulon decided that if the soldiers saw my banner going forward they would be inspired to attack and win.

'So he called out to the Basque: "If I turn and run toward the fort, will you follow me?"

'The Basque promised he would, so d'Aulon leapt into the ditch at the base of the wall and the Basque followed with the standard. I arrived on the scene at this point and, not knowing what was happening, grabbed the standard and we fought for it to and fro, shaking the banner wildly in the process. The soldiers thought I was making a signal for them to attack and win, and they turned and renewed their attack on the walls of the earthwork.

'Meanwhile, the citizens in the town saw that the attack had been renewed and set out to get into the Tourelles by building a catwalk across from the top of the city walls to the fort. They found a wooden gutter but it was three feet short so a carpenter nailed an extra length to it and they used this narrow plank to cross from the city into the fort.

'The citizens also set out to cut the main fort of the Tourelles off from the earthwork that the soldiers were attacking. To do this, they loaded a boat full of firewood, horse bones, shoes, sulphur and anything they could find that stank. They ran it under the bridge which joined the Tourelles to the bank and set it on fire. The English were devastated. The English men defending the earthwork retreated across the bridge to the Tourelles.

'Glasdale and about thirty of his best men formed a rearguard to let the others escape to the Tourelles. By the time they tried to cross the bridge themselves, the fire had taken hold and the bridge collapsed under them. Several of the men, including Glasdale were drowned. This fulfilled my prophecy that Glasdale would die unshriven but it gave me no pleasure. The English had fought very bravely and those last few men had sacrificed themselves to try to get the rest to safety. All for nothing as our soldiers and citizens stormed the Tourelles, capturing or killing all the English and setting it on fire.'

# Chapter 23: The Glorious Eighth of May

'After that we rode back into the city. All the bells were ringing and everyone was celebrating and giving thanks to God. Most people went to church to give thanks and even the older women of Orléans who had wanted to keep the French soldiers out of the town for fear of their intentions with their daughters, now welcomed them in and fed them as if they were their own sons.

'I went back to Boucher's house and a surgeon was called to dress my wound. I had not eaten all day so I had some bread soaked in wine and water. I remember that earlier in the morning before I rode out, a citizen had brought me a fish and suggested I eat it before I left. I told him to keep it for me till evening because I would bring them a godon then. Godon was what we called the English because of their habit of cursing by saying "Goddam". I don't know what happened to that fish.'

She paused as if considering the point, so I asked, 'The next day, 8 May 1429, is the one that has been celebrated ever since in Orléans. What happened on that day?'

'It seems the English believed that they could only have been beaten by someone serving the Devil. They had considered themselves, with good cause, unbeatable. They had terrorized and dominated the French in France for almost one hundred years and here, in the space of thirteen hours, the tide had turned. I must, therefore be in league with the Devil. How else could they explain it?

'Anyway, early in the morning, they pulled down their tents and lined up for battle. I was woken up and told of this development. My wound was so sore, I could not put my armour on so I wore a light suit of chain mail.

'It was a Sunday and I gave orders that no French soldier was to attack on a Sunday but if they were attacked they could defend themselves. The French army was hot for blood and wanted to finish off the English. I forbade it. I led the army out and we lined up opposite the English and stood facing each other for an hour. I had a portable altar brought out and two masses were sung. Nobody moved on either side for quite some time and then the English turned and left.'

'That was amazing. No wonder people thought you were a miracle worker.'

Joan shrugged and continued. 'La Hire, always the hot head, and about 100 horsemen did pursue the English and attacked the troops at the rear of the retreating army. They captured cannon and siege equipment. People from the city began to loot the abandoned English forts. In the meantime we found my herald Guienne still in irons but safe. The delay in sending to Paris for permission to burn him, had saved his life. It was then that I and the rest of the army returned to the city in procession. The citizens of Orléans gave us a great welcome.'

'You were their hero and you became known as the Maid of Orléans.'

'Actually, no one called me that in my lifetime. I think you'll find the term was first used over one hundred years later. I was only ever called The Maid.

Some of the documents from my time, have the words "of Orléans" added later in a different hand. But yes – the people of Orléans were very good to my family and kept faith in me even after my death. My mother went to live in Orléans and the city granted her a pension.'

I continued to push the point: 'That day, 8 May, has been celebrated in your honour in Orléans ever since. Right up to the French Revolution in 1793. It was restored again in 1803 and is still celebrated today. So, you had completed the first of the tasks you set out to accomplish. The next thing was to crown the King. Let's meet in Reims and talk about it there.'

'It wasn't quite so simple. There was quite a delay. Meet me in Tours and I'll tell you what happened next.'

'Why Tours?' I asked but she was gone.

# SECTION 6: TOURS, JARGEAU, PATAY

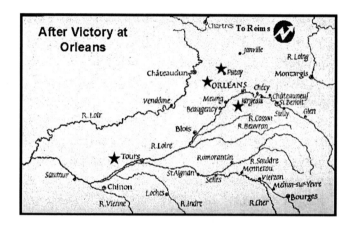

# Chapter 24: Hastening Very Slowly

'Meet me in Tours,' Joan had said. I checked the map to find Tours. It's in the opposite direction from Reims which I had assumed would be our next stop. I headed south from Orléans to Tours. I noticed on the map that it was not all that far from Chinon. I began to feel we were going around in a circle.

Still, Tours today is a great place to visit. It's even known as "The Garden of France". The people of Tours are credited with speaking the purest form of the French language in all of France. There are chateaux and castles in every direction. It was once the capital of France but long before that it was home to the Gauls and later the Romans. It gets its name from the Gallic tribe of Turones. It was in Tours in 732 AD that Charles Martel stopped the tide of northward conquests by defeating the Islamic forces. Tours is as far as they got in their push north from Spain.

Tours is also the place where the Dauphin's mistress, Agnes Sorelle, is buried. Her beautiful tomb has been moved from the church to one of the towers of the castle.

The dominant currency of Joan's time, the livre-tournois (the Tours pound), originated here too.

I headed towards the great Cathedral of St Gatien as Joan usually met me in cathedrals when possible. I passed the cedar tree that Napoleon Bonaparte had planted here, and gazed up – and up - at the towering western front of the cathedral. The cathedral was here in Joan's day and I tried to imagine what it must have looked like to her. The lowest stages of the two towers would have been there but the flamboyant upper sections were added some time later in the fifteenth century.

The site had been occupied by a chapel and a basilica and had been destroyed and rebuilt several times. An earlier cathedral had been burnt down in 1166 during a quarrel between – you guessed it – the English King Henry II and the French King Louis VII. The present day cathedral was begun in 1170 and has been added to repeatedly over the centuries.

I sat in the back row of the cathedral and studied the stained glass windows. They are among the most beautiful in France and date from medieval times. In one window, St Martin is shown reluctantly becoming the second Bishop of Tours. That is certainly the face of an unhappy man. Was the realism intended? No way of knowing. I was suddenly glad to be so unexpectedly in Tours. Reims could wait. I was enjoying the detour.

Joan, however, had not as I was soon to learn. I heard her voice before she appeared beside me.

'I see you like the place,' she commented without greeting.

'I do but why did you come here? Surely the thing to do after the victory at Orléans would be to crown the king in Reims.'

'Yes, that was my urgent desire at the time. I had to wait a while till my wound healed and then I went to meet up with the Dauphin. He came to Tours to meet me. I arrived first and when I heard he was on his way, I rode out to meet him.'

I moved along the pew so she could sit beside me and said to her, 'People who were there reported that he greeted you so enthusiastically that they thought he was about to kiss you.'

Joan laughed. 'Yes. When I rode up to him, I bowed very low in the saddle. He was my king, after all. He told me to sit erect and ride with him. I was honoured. Sometimes it seemed so unreal. I was a farm girl, a peasant from Domremy and yet these things were happening to me.'

I looked at her with some surprise. 'I'd say you had earned his gratitude and respect with all you did at Orléans. But I have read a translation of the letter he wrote to the towns that were loyal to him, telling them of the victory at Orléans. Although he goes into great detail of the strategy and battles, he mentions you almost as an aside. Not exactly overflowing with gratitude or even recognition of what you had done.'

Joan bit her lip and said nothing. Her eyes moistened so I went on to a subject I thought would be a pleasant memory for her.

'So when did you head off to Reims?'

'We didn't. Charles was in no hurry. There was disagreement among those he listened to as to what should happen next. I wanted to take him straight to Reims to be crowned. Others thought we should drive the English out of Normandy before we went to Reims. Still others wanted to re-take the towns along the Loire River that were held by the English. These included Jargeau, Meung and Beaugency. They were strategic towns which the English had established as bases before they began the siege of Orléans. Some people, including the Dauphin, thought they should ask me what my voices said should be done. No one did ask me though – at least not till several days later.

'While I was with the Dauphin in Tours, the army under the command of Dunois (my old friend the Bastard of Orléans), Poton de Saintrailles and Maréchal de Saint Sévère, had attacked the town of Jargeau. They failed to take the town partly because the river was high and the ditches surrounding the town were full of water. They did kill the captain of the town, Sir Henry Bisset, in a skirmish though.

'Meanwhile, I was cooling my heels with the court. Not my lifestyle. All that fawning and gossip and intrigue and treachery. Give me a good hard battle any day. The Dauphin asked me to go with him to his castle in Loches. Of course, I went. I wasn't letting him out of my sight until he agreed to go to Reims.

'The Bastard joined me at Loches. Thank God for a good honest soldier to talk to.

'After we arrived at the castle in Loches, I took the Bastard with me to find the Dauphin. He was in his private room talking with his confessor and my lord Christophe de Harcourt. I knocked on the door and as soon as I was allowed in, I fell on my knees in front of the Dauphin and threw my arms around his legs. I was desperate. I knew that my time was limited. My voices had told me that much.

'I said to him "Noble Dauphin, do not take such long and copious counsel, but come as quickly as you can to receive a worthy coronation."

'It was then that Christophe spoke up. "Is this what your Counsel said should be done?" he asked.

"Yes, yes." I replied. "The matter is urgent."

'Christophe continued, "Will you not tell us here in the King's presence, in what manner your Counsel speaks to you?"

'The Dauphin then also said, "Joan, let it please you to say what he demands in the presence of those who are here."

'I was a bit embarrassed to be revealing things so intimate and dear to me but I told them that when people would not follow the commands I had received from my Counsellor, I would go off by myself and pray to God. Then I would hear a voice saying "Go, child of God, go, go! Go, and I will help you."

'I also told them that when I heard this voice, I felt a great joy. Just talking to them brought the feeling back and they could see how rapt I was. I think they were a little embarrassed too.

'Finally, the Dauphin decided he would go to Reims but that some of the towns along the Loire had to be taken from the English first.'

'It must have been very frustrating for you,' I said. Joan said nothing.

# Chapter 25: The Fall of Jargeau

I went back to studying the sad glass face of St Martin.

Finally Joan continued. 'One thing that pleased me greatly was the appointment of my *beau duc*, d'Alençon, to Lieutenant-General. He was put in charge of the army.

'D'Alençon and I returned to Orléans on 9 June – almost a month to the day since our victory. The citizens were as warm and welcoming as ever. We used Orléans for our base over the next week. After spending a night in Orléans we rode out accompanied by 600 lances. We spent the night in a wood and were joined the following morning by Dunois and Florent d'Illiers with their men. There was some considerable discussion as to whether or not to attack Jargeau again. You remember that Dunois already had one go at it and failed.

'Jargeau was occupied by a force led by the Duke of Suffolk and his two brothers, the de la Poles. We also knew that Sir John Falstaff was on his way from Paris with supplies and reinforcements for Suffolk and his men.

'Some of the captains thought Falstaff should be stopped first and then we could attack Jargeau. I listened to them for a while and finally I lost patience. I told them plainly that God was on their side and we were going to succeed in capturing Jargeau. I added that if I didn't think this, I would be back minding sheep rather than put myself at such risk. That shook them up a bit and we were soon on the road to Jargeau with the intention of capturing at least the outer suburbs before nightfall.

'We were all in high spirits until the English saw us coming and came out to do battle. Our troops faltered and looked set to back off but I held my standard high and charged forward alone towards the enemy. Our soldiers took heart at that and followed me with great shouts.

'We captured the outskirts of the town and the English withdrew into the walled section. We camped there for the night and I went and stood beneath the wall of the town and called out to the English.

"Surrender the place to the King of Heaven and the gentle King Charles, and you can go off, but otherwise we will massacre you."

'They didn't even answer me.

'The next morning was 12 June. The captains were again gathering to discuss what to do next when they learnt that La Hire had begun private negotiations with Suffolk. They were very angry and sent for him to come back. I've no idea why he did that. He was my companion in arms and had been with me from the beginning. Part of it seems to be that Suffolk had refused to deal with a woman – me – but was prepared to talk to La Hire.

'The captains continued their discussions and d'Alençon felt it was not wise to continue the attack.

'I said to him: "Forward, gentle Duke, forward to the attack. Don't doubt it is now the time that pleases God. Act, and God will act! Don't be afraid. Remember I promised your wife I'd bring you back safe and sound."

'He drew courage from my words and it was decided to attack at once. We charged the walls and the English were firing at us from the top of the walls.

I interrupted her. 'This is the occasion on which you saved d'Alençon's life, isn't it? You ran to his side and said to him: "Move from this place or that cannon on the rampart will kill you." He moved away and a few minutes later another captain was killed by that gun on that spot.'

'Yes, that did happen. It gave d'Alençon even more confidence to follow me and later when Suffolk tried to negotiate a settlement with him, he refused to listen to him but urged his troops to keep fighting.'

Again I interrupted. 'It was at this point that you were hit by a rock.'

'Mmm. That's true. I was climbing one of the scaling ladders with my banner in my hand when a rock hit the banner and then hit my helmet. It knocked me backwards off the ladder and I fell to the ground.

'I knew how important it was for my banner to be seen by the troops so I leapt up and shouted: "Friends, friends! Up! Up! Our Lord has condemned the English; they will be ours within the hour."

'When our soldiers saw me get up again and heard me shouting, they attacked with even greater energy and scaled the walls, swarming into the town.'

'It's amazing you weren't knocked out by that rock.'

'I was wearing a *chapeline* that day. It was a kind of tin hat worn by the men who lead the charge on walls of towns.

'As our men entered the town, Suffolk and his men tried to retreat across the river. Our soldiers went after them. Sadly, it turned into a massacre. Suffolk decided to surrender for ransom. The closest Frenchman to him was a squire called Guillaume Regnault, and when Suffolk found that he was not a knight, he immediately knighted him and then surrendered to him. Regnault would have cheerfully accepted the honour and the ransom.

'There were about 700 Englishmen in Jargeau when we attacked. Only about fifty survived. The rest were massacred. Our soldiers were out for blood and there was no stopping them. Not a lot was said about this at the time because the knights and nobles were the ones that survived but the judges at my trial picked it up and used it against me later.'

'This is the horror of war, any war, in any age,' I responded. 'After Orléans the English were convinced you were a sorceress, an agent of the Devil. How else could you have beaten them so well and so often, or so they saw it?'

Joan nodded. 'After winning at Jargeau, d'Alençon and I rode back to Orléans. There I was presented with a red cloak and a green tunic on behalf of the Duke of Orléans who was still held captive in England. Red and green were the colours of his coat of arms.

# Chapter 26: On the Front Foot at Last

'After a day and a half in Orléans, I urged d'Alençon to get moving again. On the second evening there. I told him I wanted to pay a visit to Meung the next afternoon. That was one of the other towns on the Loire occupied by the English. I told him to have the army ready to start at that time.'

I couldn't help commenting on this. 'D'Alençon was a royal prince and commander in chief of the army. That sounds pretty high handed of you to be giving him orders.'

Joan did not take offence but explained. 'My *beau duc* and I were friends. We enjoyed each other's company and I was very fond of him. He believed in me and trusted me. The next day, at Meung, we contented ourselves with giving the English a fright. We took the English garrison on the bridge but left the town alone and continued on to Beaugency.

'When the English saw us coming, they retreated into the castle. I should say at this point, the English commander in Beaugency was Talbot and he and several of his men took the opportunity to escape from the town before we actually attacked it. The next day, 16 June, the battle went on till midnight and ended with the English surrendering. We allowed them to retreat to Meung on the condition that they did not fight again for ten days.'

I interrupted her. 'That's a bit difficult for us to understand these days.'

Joan considered my comment and finally replied, 'I guess war and battles were much more personal and close up than the way you fight today.

'During the day, the Constable of France, Artur, Comte de Richemont arrived with a large number of troops. Artur had fallen out with the Dauphin who disliked him intensely. He was a blunt coarse soldier, it's true and Charles had not wanted him to be Constable of France in the first place. The Dauphin's mother-in-law, Yolanda of Aragon, had arranged the appointment. Artur had in turn appointed Trémoille to Charles's council. Big mistake. Once in power, Trémoille banished Artur from the court and set about maintaining his own influence over the Dauphin.

'D'Alençon was not sure if we should greet him in a friendly way or not. I thought we should ride out and fight him but the captains talked me out of it. I asked d'Alençon, the Bastard, Gui de Laval and his brother to accompany me to meet Artur. We rode out and met the approaching force. Artur and I dismounted and walked towards each other. I think everyone else held their breaths to see what was going to happen next.

'As was customary, I knelt and embraced his knees. Artur turned out to be quite a reasonable man.

'He said to me: "Joan, I hear you want to fight me. I don't know if you come from God or not. If you do come from God I don't fear you because God knows my good intentions. If you come from the Devil, I fear you even less."

'I stood up, we mounted our horses and we all rode back to Beaugency. That night the Constable's men provided the night sentinels. This was the custom too.

The sentinels were drawn from the ranks of the latest arrivals.

'At dawn, we let the English leave Beaugency. As they were going, a messenger rode up with the news that Talbot who had escaped from Beaugency earlier, and Falstaff were on their way with 5,000 men to help their countrymen from Beaugency. Several of the French captains immediately decided on retreat but I wouldn't hear of it. I turned to Artur, who as I said had brought a large number of men with him. I had every intention of making use of them.

'I said to him: "Ah, good constable, I was not responsible for your coming, but since you have come, you shall be welcome."

'Then to my own captains I said: "In God's name, we must fight them. If they were hanging in the clouds, we should get them, for God has sent them to us to punish them." And so they agreed to stay and join us in the fight.'

# Chapter 27: The Battle of Patay

'Artur rode forward towards the English with his banner waving and his men following. I and the French army followed. This was a momentous occasion; it was the first time the French army had taken the offensive in battle and it was the turning point in the war. The French army ranged itself in battle positions as the English army approached. The English sent two heralds to us to say they had three knights who would fight our army if we had the courage for it. In turn, we sent an equally contemptuous reply: "Find somewhere to rest for tonight as it's already late but tomorrow, God and Our Lady willing, we will see you at closer quarters."

'The English retired and camped near Meung and we spent the night in Beaugency.

'Next day, was a strange situation. Neither army knew where the other army was. At that time, the countryside in the area near Patay was very heavily wooded and the two armies could not see each other. I was with D'Alencon, the Bastard and Artur.

'D'Alençon asked, "Joan, what should we do?"

"Have all of you good spurs?" I replied.

"What! Should we turn our backs and run away?"

"No" I said, "It will be the English who will turn their backs and you will need spurs to pursue them."

'I did not play a large part in the battle that followed. I remained in the rear. If this was to be a pitched battle in the open, they wanted me safely out of the way. They probably thought I'd disagree with their plans as I had in the past.

'Several scouts were sent out to locate the English army and during their search they startled a deer, a large stag. The animal bounded into the English advance guard and the English could not help but cheer as they do when they are hunting. It was their downfall because we heard them and attacked immediately before they could organize themselves for battle. Falstaff saw what was happening and lead his men to help the advance guard. When they saw Falstaff galloping towards them, they assumed that all was lost and that he was in retreat. They too immediately took flight and left the rest of the army to its fate. Falstaff wanted to rejoin the main army and fight against us but his fellow officers persuaded him that the battle was lost and it was best to retire.

'The number of English killed was around two thousand. We didn't keep exact numbers in those days. Many of their nobles and commanders were taken prisoner including Talbot. The English foot soldiers were massacred because they were not worth taking for their ransoms. On the French side, there were hardly any men killed at all. It was reported that only three died.

'I arrived on the battlefield as the slaughter of the English was going on. One of our soldiers was bringing in a group of English prisoners and suddenly knocked one of them on the head and left him for dead. I was horrified. I remember I dismounted and went to the dying Englishman. I held his head and tried to comfort him. I received his confession and held him till he died.'

Joan paused and there were tears in her eyes. Then she continued.

'And so the battle of Patay was over by two o'clock in the afternoon. It was 18 June 1429.

'I heard later that Falstaff had consistently opposed Talbot's plans to attack us on the grounds that they did not have sufficient strength of numbers. Since Talbot was in command, Falstaff had been forced to go along with the disastrous battle. He managed to return to the Duke of Bedford to report the news of their defeat. Bedford apparently flew into a rage and stripped Falstaff of his Order of the Garter but later restored it when he realized that Falstaff's advice to Talbot had been wise all along.

'Most of the troops spent that night camped on the battlefield. D'Alençon, Artur and I went into the town of Patay. Talbot was brought before us and d'Alençon taunted him with the words: "You did not think this morning that such a thing would happen to you?" To give Talbot his due, he answered philosophically enough: "It is the fortune of war."

'The next day, we went back to Orléans. The people were celebrating the victories at Beaugency and Patay and everyone was in high spirits. The citizens expected the Dauphin would come to Orléans and join the festivities. They decorated the town especially in expectation of his arrival. He didn't come.

'The Dauphin had taken the court to Sully. I went there to see him and tried to persuade him to go to Reims for his coronation. He kept putting me off and told me not to be so concerned about him. I remember I burst into tears because I could not convince him to act. But let's go to Reims now.'

*At last,* I thought as she disappeared.

# SECTION 7: REIMS

# Chapter 28: Dauphin or King? What's in a Name?

The town of Reims is just a pleasant train trip north east from Paris. The town gets its name (almost unpronounceable in French) from the Rémi, a Gallic tribe who lived there before Roman times.

It was a cold, cloudy, windy day in October – thoroughly miserable - but a short walk from the station took me to the cathedral. In France, Reims Cathedral has a similar significance as Westminster Abbey has in England. It was here that French Kings were crowned.

I sat at an outdoor café nearby and watched the carousel in the pedestrian mall in front of me. I wrapped my shivering fingers around the hot cup and took my first sip of steaming coffee. As I gave a sigh of sheer comfort and pleasure, Joan arrived.

I was pleased to see her. This was the town of her second greatest triumph. The town where she fulfilled her promise to have the Dauphin crowned King of France. I began the interview with that fact in mind.

'Joan, why do you call Charles "the Dauphin" and not King?'

Joan began her explanation. 'Everyone in France in those days knew that a king was not a king until he had been anointed by the Holy Oil that was kept in the city of Reims. It was believed that the Holy Spirit entered the King through the Holy Oil and, from then on, he was King in God's sight.

'The Dauphin had never been officially crowned. He'd never knelt before the altar in Reims and made his kingly vows to God. Nor had he received God's blessing through the medium of God's bishop.'

I did not pursue this further but later checked the origins of the title "dauphin". It began as a given name in the twelfth century and was later misinterpreted as a title finally becoming a title applied only to the heir to the throne.

'What's the story behind the Holy Oil?' I asked.

'The legend is that a tiny bottle of Holy Oil was brought to Reims by a white dove 1300 years before my lifetime. It was never allowed to leave Reims – well it did leave once but that was a special occasion and required the Pope's permission. Since the oil could not leave Reims, Kings had to go there to be anointed and crowned.'

I nodded. 'I see why you were so keen to get Charles to Reims even though strategically it would have been better to attack Paris which was in enemy hands, before the English re-enforcements arrived.'

'I know. I know. Militarily, that would have been the smart thing to do and I've had long enough to regret it. However, for the reason I have given you, it was crucial to get Charles to Reims. All of France knew it. Even the English knew it.'

'So did you head for Reims?'

Joan shook her head. Even now there were tears of frustration in her eyes and I saw her lips tighten as she chose her words.

'Charles' advisers were counseling him to be careful. There were a number of enemy-held towns still between us and Reims and they thought we should attack those first to make it safe for the Dauphin to get there. Charles himself said he had no money to pay troops and this was his reason for doing nothing.'

I interrupted again. 'This excuse wouldn't hold up for long because, as you mentioned earlier, men were flocking in from all over France. They were willing to fight for Charles without any pay. Even gentlemen enlisted as ordinary soldiers and archers, mounted on ponies because they personally could not afford the warhorses and trappings that their status entitled them to.'

Joan nodded and I continued.

'I've read that the army swelled to 12,000 men willing to fight for Charles but they said they would follow the Maid wherever she would lead them. Your tremendous popularity must have made a few people in the court very nervous.'

'Yes – I mentioned earlier that there were always intrigues and struggles to gain the Dauphin's attention and trust. I've also mentioned Charles' main favourite at the time, La Trémoille. You'll remember he got rid of the Constable of France, Artur the one who came to our aid at Patay. After that battle, we thought the Dauphin would take Artur back but Trémoille saw to it that the Constable and all his men were sent packing. A terrible waste when we needed every man we could get.'

'Where was the Dauphin at this stage?'

'He had moved the court yet again, this time to the castle at Gien just a little upriver from Sully. All his advisers were with him, whispering in his ear about the dangers ahead. At first he sent for the Queen to join him so that she could go with him to the coronation. Then he sent her back to Bourges saying it was too dangerous for her. I begged and pleaded with him to get going but he wouldn't budge.

'After about a week of delay, I was so frustrated and angry, I went and camped in the fields for a couple of nights and left Charles to his conniving courtiers. This seems to have stirred him to action because he suddenly announced he was ready to go and away we went. It was 30th June 1429. I rode beside him and our army, although large, had very little to eat as Charles was unable to do more than give each man a few francs.

'The first town we arrived at was Auxerre on 1 July. The townsfolk closed their gates and refused to let us in. They said they would give the same obedience to the king as the rest of the cities on the route would do. These were the cities of Troyes, Châlons and Reims.

It was a deliberately cheeky response but understandable. Auxerres belonged to the Duke of Burgundy. As you know, he was the leader of the main French party supporting the English invasion. The second reason they were reluctant to let us in was fear. The citizens could only imagine what a large and hungry army would do once they were let loose in the town.

They had obviously given it some thought because they came up with the idea of offering La Trémoille a bribe if he would prevent the king from attacking. They in turn would provide food for the troops. Trémoille personally received 2,000 écus[7] and convinced Charles to call a temporary truce. I was furious and so were

---

[7] The eçu, was one of several forms of currency in use at the time. It fluctuated in value but was probably worth approximately the same as the livre-tournois mentioned earlier.

many of the other captains. The city was not well defended and we believed we could have taken it easily. But done is done and we stayed there for three days trading for food.'

'So then you set out for Reims?'

'No, there were still a couple of towns along the way. The next one we came to was Troyes.'

# Chapter 29: Oh Brother! Troyes Again

'We've talked about Troyes or the Treaty of Troyes before, haven't we? And this is where you met Brother Richard.'

'Yes. The Treaty of Troyes was the ugly arrangement made by the King of France (the Dauphin's father) or more to the point by Isabeau, the Dauphin's mother, the King of England and the Duke of Burgundy. As I told you, that Treaty named Henry V of England as heir to the French throne and specifically excluded the "so-called" Dauphin as heir. It stated that no treaties or peace were to be made with him. It implied that he was not really the son of the King of France. The suggestion that he was illegitimate was endorsed and perhaps even suggested by his mother. The Treaty also contained a clause arranging for the marriage of Henry V to Catherine, daughter of the French King and Queen, the Dauphin's own sister.'

'What a mess!'

Joan actually laughed at my amazement then continued her story. 'When the Dauphin and I arrived with our army in front of the gates of Troyes, the people understandably thought he would take his revenge on them. He sent them a letter saying that the past should be forgotten and forgiven. I think the townspeople's sympathies were with the Dauphin. They crowded the city walls to have a look at us but made no attempt to attack us. There was a garrison of soldiers posted in the town and they were stirring for a fight. They fired a couple of cannon shots at us but luckily they didn't hit anyone. They came out of the gate but I think it was all bravado because we outnumbered them so much they just retreated back into the city.

'The Bishop of Troyes came out to speak to the Dauphin. He confirmed that it was mainly the soldiers who wouldn't open the gates and, if he could have some time, he thought he could persuade the townspeople to open the gates in peace.

'The problem was that our army was close to starving. We had a stroke of luck though because there was a preacher in Troyes who had made quite a name for himself in Paris. Brother Richard he called himself and he preached the coming of the Anti-Christ.'

'Could you just briefly explain what that means please.'

'It's based on a belief that one person will be born on earth that is the embodiment of evil and will bring disaster. In Brother Richard's sermons which often lasted for several hours, he had told the people of Troyes 'Sow, good people, sow beans in abundance for He who is to come will come before long.' He was probably talking about the Anti-Christ but the people took him literally and planted lots of beans in the fields. Our soldiers survived by eating them.'

'You met Brother Richard didn't you?'

'Yes, he came out to meet me. In the meantime, the Dauphin held numerous meetings with his advisers and captains. After several days, the Dauphin held his last meeting and the majority there wanted to retreat. I was not at the meetings but I was called after they had made the decision to retreat. They asked my opinion of their decision.

'I knelt to the Dauphin and said to him: "Noble Dauphin, command your people to come and besiege the city of Troyes, and drag out your debates no longer. For in God's name, within three days I will lead you into the city of Troyes, by love, force or courage, and that false Burgundy will be quite thunderstruck."

'The Chancellor said: "Joan, if it were certain that we would have the city in six days, we would of course wait."

'That was enough for me. I left them to their debating and set about preparing to besiege the city. I got everyone to work, even the squires and knights, bringing up material needed to attack the city.'

She paused a moment and I commented, 'Dunois, the Bastard of Orléans, told the rehabilitation hearing that: "The positions she took up were so admirable that the most famous and experienced captains would not have made so good a plan of battle."'

Joan looked a bit embarrassed at this praise and shrugged her shoulders.

'It seemed mostly common sense to me. Anyway, the people of Troyes watched the preparations from the top of their walls and decided that they didn't want to fight at all. The next morning, just as I had the trumpets sound the attack, they surrendered.

'I went into the city and organized the Dauphin's entry. It was done with all the pomp of a gala entrance. I rode beside Charles, carrying my banner. The people all turned out to greet us.'

'Let's get back to Brother Richard. They mention him in your trial so perhaps you could tell us a bit about him now.'

Joan hesitated then continued. 'All right. As I said, he came out of the town to meet me. The people of Troyes sent him out to check if I was from God or the Devil. He made the sign of the cross and sprinkled holy water as he came near me. He looked a bit nervous so to help him relax I made a joke of it.

'I said to him: "Approach boldly. I shall not fly away."

'He fell on his knees in front of me so I did the same to him. I never wanted people to idolize me or treat me like some saintly being. I was just a woman with a mission and a very strong belief in what I was doing. Brother Richard went back into the city and began preaching to the people that they should accept the Dauphin as King. He made claims about me that I would never have claimed for myself.'

'What sort of claims?'

'He said I had as much power to know God's secrets as any saint in paradise and that I could, if I wanted to, make the King's army enter over the walls in any way I wanted.

'He came with me to Reims and even stood near me at the coronation. He held my banner when I got tired. He also was my confessor for a time. But, Brother Richard preferred to be the centre of attention and he "collected" a couple of other women who were supposed to be visionaries. One in particular was Catherine de la Rochelle, and he tried to get the Dauphin to make use of her visions. I didn't approve of her and told him so. She was a fraud and she was trying to trick the Dauphin.'

'Didn't you try to prove her visions were false?'

'Yes. She claimed that a white lady came to her at night and advised her on all manner of things including peace-making with the Duke of Burgundy. I told her that the only peace to be made with him would be at the point of a lance. I said I would spend the night with her so that I too could see the white lady. We sat up all night and I finally fell asleep, more out of boredom than anything. Next morning, Catherine assured me the white lady had visited her while I was asleep and that she had been unable to wake me up.

'Next day, I made sure I slept all day, and that night, I spent again with Catherine. I kept her awake till dawn but no white lady showed up. I told her to go back to her husband and look after her house and children.'

'I gather you and Brother Richard didn't get on with each other after that.'

'No. Enough of him. Let's move on.'

'The next town on the way was Châlons. How did the people there react to you?'

'They welcomed us in to the town and we stayed there one night. The Dauphin had written to all the towns known to be loyal to him, announcing his forthcoming coronation. People had begun flocking towards Reims for the event and many of them were staying in Châlons on the way.

'This town was the closest I had been to my home in Domremy since I left and it was here that I met four or five people from Domremy. There was my godfather, Jean Morel. It was great to see him and I gave him the red dress I had been wearing when I left home. There was also Gerardin d'Epinal and I spoke with him and a couple of others. One of them asked me if I was afraid and I remember I told them that I feared nothing except treachery.'

'You certainly came up against plenty of that.'

Joan said nothing but again there were tears in her eyes.

I quickly changed the subject. 'So now you could head straight for Reims.'

Joan shook her head and for the first time there was a trace of bitterness in her voice. 'You think?' she said. 'Oh no! By now we had all Charles' advisers traveling with us including La Trémoille. You could always count on them to slow us down in more ways than one. We did not have any siege equipment with us and Charles, ever cautious, felt it was unwise to proceed to Reims in case the town defied him. We stopped at the castle of Sept Saulx, twelve miles from Reims. On 4 July 1429, Charles wrote a letter to the people of Reims inviting them to send an embassy to him.

'The citizens of Reims were playing it both ways and waiting to see if the Duke of Burgundy was going to make them a better offer, so they asked for more time to consult. I opposed the delay and urged the Dauphin to go forward.

'I said to him "Doubt not. Advance boldly and fear nothing."

'On 16 July, the officials of the town came out to Sept Saulx and presented him with the keys to the city and offered him "full and entire obedience as their sovereign". We entered Reims on the same day and all the townspeople came out to greet us with cheers.

'That was on a Saturday and by tradition a coronation had to be performed on a Sunday. Rather than wait another week, it was decided to go ahead with the ceremony on the following day. What a rush to get things ready but it all came together in time.'

# Chapter 30: The Crowning Moment

'What was the ceremony like?'

'It started with Charles entering the cathedral of Reims at 3 a.m. to keep the traditional vigil through the night. At 9 a.m. the ritual began. Four horsemen in full armour rode to the Church of Saint Rémi where the Holy Oil was kept. One of them was my old comrade in arms, Gilles de Rais. You now know him as Bluebeard. The abbot of Saint Rémi carried the Holy Oil on horseback and, accompanied by the four knights, rode into the cathedral right up to the choir and presented the oil to the Archbishop of Reims. Charles then took the coronation oath to protect the Church and the people and to govern with justice and mercy. Alençon then knighted him. He was anointed with the Holy Oil and crowned. Everyone cheered and the trumpets made the vaults of the church shake.'

'One of the most extraordinary things about that coronation was that you stood by the King's side the whole time and you were holding your banner.'

'Yes, that's correct. It was a great moment for me. The ceremony lasted five hours so it was quite a lengthy ordeal for everyone. That's why I let Brother Richard hold my banner occasionally. When the ceremony ended, I knelt in front of Charles and embraced his legs.

'I was crying with joy and I said to him, "Gentle King, now is done God's pleasure, Who willed that I raise the siege of Orléans and I bring you to this city of Reims to receive your holy sacring showing that you are true king and him to whom the kingdom of God should belong."

'The other wonderful thing about the coronation was that my father was there. I hadn't seen him since I left Domremy. He was at the coronation and he stayed in an inn called *The Striped Donkey*. The city of Reims paid for his accommodation and the King gave me sixty *livres* to give him as a present. Although we did not have much time together, it was wonderful to see him and to ask his forgiveness for running away from home. My Uncle Durand Lassois was there too. It was good to see him. Remember he was the first person who believed in me and took me to see Robert de Baudricourt?'

'There's a plaque on the site of that inn that says both your parents were there. You didn't mention your mother.'

'No, she wasn't there so that is not correct. Sadly, because it would have been wonderful to see her. Let's move on.'

'Did Charles offer you any reward for all that you had done for him?'

'Not exactly but I did ask him for a favour. I asked that the villages of Domremy and Greux be exempted from taxes forever and he signed an ordnance to ensure it.'

'How did the Duke of Burgundy react to Charles being crowned?'

'Not well. I had sent him an invitation to the coronation but he did not come. After the ceremony was finished, I wrote another letter to him begging him to make a longstanding peace with Charles and to shed no more blood.'

'Charles was certainly in the stronger position now that he was crowned and so many towns had changed over to his side.'

'That's right and that is why I chose that moment to write to the Duke of Burgundy. He had sent two messengers to Reims as it turned out and they arrived on the day of the coronation. They met with Charles in secret. I was kept out of the discussions and from his new position of strength, my noble Dauphin now King Charles, concluded a peace treaty of two weeks! In return for a two-week truce, the Duke of Burgundy offered to hand over Paris to him.

'The negotiations were a fraud. They were meant to buy time for the Burgundians and the English. The Duke of Bedford had sent for re-enforcements from England and 3,500 men were already traveling towards

Paris before the negotiations even began. We should have attacked Paris and taken it straight after the coronation but my King spent four precious days talking to Burgundy's lying emissaries.'

'Well, you succeeded magnificently in your mission. All this in only five months since you had left Domremy. It was amazing.'

Joan sighed.

'Yes. If only I had stopped there. But from the moment Charles negotiated with the Duke of Burgundy, I was on a downward slope. I remember telling the Bastard and the Archbishop of Reims that I wished God would let me lay down my weapons and go home to my mother and father.'

'So what happened?' I asked, shivering in the cool air of the sidewalk café. It had begun to rain.

'Let's go into the cathedral. It's more sheltered and I'll tell you the rest of the story.'

We walked into the cathedral of Reims and down the aisle. As I approached the altar, I noticed a small statue of Joan tucked over to the right behind a pillar. It was fairly primitively sculpted and seemed a very small tribute indeed to the momentous event she had brought about in this place. Joan paid no attention to it and sat down. Grateful to be out of the wind, I joined her and she went straight on as though we had not interrupted our discussion.

'La Trémoille was there in Charles' ear. The Archbishop of Reims too. They were counseling him to negotiate at all costs. Avoid a confrontation with Burgundy and England. La Trémoille had a kinsman in the Burgundian court and I sometimes wonder about that influence. In signing this two-week truce, Charles had condemned us to two weeks of inactivity while the English and Burgundians re-enforced Paris.'

'Sounds fairly stupid on the part of your King, if you don't mind my saying so.'

Again Joan sighed.

'That was Charles. He wasn't much of a fighter. He preferred to spend his time at court, living a life of leisure and wishing his problems would disappear.

'We finally left Reims together after four days of putting it off and arrived at Soissons two days later. Instead of heading straight for Paris, the King took us on a wander around the countryside avoiding the hard decisions. He would not even enter the important town of Compiègne although it was prepared to surrender without resistance. By 2 August we arrived at the town of Provins where we stayed for three days.'

'You were very uncritical of him even in these circumstances. There's a letter you wrote to the people of Reims at that time which gives an indication of your feelings. In that letter, you promise never to abandon them as long as you live.'

Joan said nothing so I continued. 'You referred to the truce the King had made with the Duke of Burgundy but you said you were not in favour of truces entered into in this way and that you did not know if you would keep it. If you did keep the truce it would only be to preserve the King's honour. You stated you would keep the King's army together in readiness in case at the end of the two-week truce, the Duke does not keep his word and surrender Paris.

'How right you were. They had no intention of handing over Paris in spite of their promises.'

# SECTION 8: PARIS

# Chapter 31: A Woman Disordered and Defamed

Joan continued her story and her voice was sad. 'Charles was intent on retreating towards the Loire even though we had the upper hand at that stage. He intended to cross the River Seine by a bridge at Bray and head south away from Paris. When his advance guard arrived at the bridge, they found it had been captured by the English the previous night and the route was closed. To my relief, Charles was forced back towards Paris and stopped at Château Thierry. It was then that the Duke of Bedford wrote to Charles, a very rude letter calling doubt on his legitimacy as King even though he had been crowned.'

'That letter also was even ruder about you, wasn't it?'

'Yes, he called me a "woman disordered and defamed, being in man's clothes and of dissolute conduct". He also challenged Charles to meet him and his army to do battle.'

'I would have thought that Charles would have been stung by the insults to both himself and you, enough to take a tougher line with Bedford.'

'Sadly, no. Charles continued to negotiate with Bedford, usually without my knowledge or even without telling his commanders. Meanwhile, Bedford had plenty of time to fortify Paris and on 14 August, he and his army headed towards Senlis which is north of Paris. On the way, they stopped at the village of

Montepilloy then continued to a little village called Notre Dame de la Victoire.

'It was a Sunday and on the same day, our army arrived at Montepilloy and camped in a wood nearby. I was there with the Duke of Alençon and other captains and commanders. The armies were so close but, except for a few skirmishes, there was no battle.

'The next morning, we prepared for battle and moved towards the English camp. The English had set themselves up with the river behind them and ditches and stakes in front of them. They stayed behind these makeshift fortifications and made no effort to come out and fight.

'Finally, I rode right up to their position and banged my standard on their fortifications. I called out to them to come out and fight. They would not.

'All during the day there were small skirmishes between groups from either side. It was a terribly hot day and the dust was incredible. With the various skirmishes going on, the ground was trampled and the dust rose up so that it was hard to tell who was on your side and who was not. Alençon sent the English a challenge and told them that we would withdraw and give them time to set themselves up for battle but they refused.

'By nightfall, we returned to camp. King Charles had spent the day at Montepilloy but when there was no battle, he spent the night at Crépy which was more comfortably set up for him. In the end the two armies withdrew and no battle was fought. Bedford went back to Paris.

'The next day negotiations continued with the Duke of Burgundy. The Archbishop of Reims led the French negotiators to make peace with the Duke. They were instructed by Charles to make many concessions with very little being asked in return.'

'That was extraordinary given that many of the towns in Burgundy were ready to surrender to Charles and call him King,' I commented.

'Yes, somehow Charles never seemed willing or able to take advantage of the tremendous popularity and loyalty our victories had inspired – at least not in my lifetime. Anyway, while all this was going on, Bedford was strengthening Paris with his English soldiers in the belief that we would attack it.

'It was at this point that you received a letter from the Count d'Armagnac, wasn't it?'

'Yes. I was about to mount my horse when the Count's messenger arrived. This Count d'Armagnac was not a member of the Armagnac party and was actually a supporter of the Burgundians and English. His letter asked me which of the three rival popes of the time ought to be obeyed and would I ask guidance from Jesus Christ and let him know. A crowd had gathered around and was threatening to throw the messenger into the river. I quickly dictated a letter saying that I was busy making war and when I was at rest in Paris, I would make enquiries and let him know. It was a comment I should never have made. It set me up for charges of incredible presumption at my trial. It was done in haste in difficult circumstances.' She bowed her head and said nothing further.

I contributed what I knew of the next part of her story. 'Charles had moved to Compiègne and seemed content to settle in. What did you do?'

'I said to the Duke of Alençon "Call your men and the other captains to arms. I want to see Paris closer than I have seen it."

'We took the army to St Denis on the outskirts of Paris. This was August 23. D'Alençon went back and forth to the King to persuade him to join us. Finally on August 28, Charles came as close as Senlis.

'He continued to negotiate with the Duke of Burgundy and on 28 August an armistice was agreed to. This "allowed" the French to attack Paris but also "allowed" the Duke of Burgundy to go to the aid of the defenders of Paris.'

'That's peculiar. So Charles was to allow his army to attack the English in Paris but agrees as part of the armistice, that the Duke of Burgundy can send soldiers to fight against the French army. What sort of a truce is that?'

Joan did not speak for some time. She drew a deep breath and continued. 'To sweeten the deal for the Duke of Burgundy, Charles even offered to "lend" him the town of Compiègne. The citizens of Compiègne refused to be "lent". In the meantime, we in the army attacking Paris knew nothing of the Treaty. It was kept a secret.

# Chapter 32: Betrayal by a King

'Paris, in those days, was the largest city in the Christian world and was neither easy to defend nor to attack. We took a number of English strongholds near the city and prepared to attack the city itself.

'On 8 September, we began the final attack. There was heavy artillery fire from the walls but it did little damage. There were two ditches in front of the city walls, one dry and the other filled with water. We need to know how deep the water was so I dismounted and went down into the first ditch. A few of the captains, including Gilles de Rais came with me.

'As we did so, the French army charged the length of the wall. I put my lance into the water to see how deep it was. At the same time I called out to the defenders on the walls to surrender to the King of France or they would all be killed.

'A cross-bowman on the walls shouted back at me, "Will we, you bloody tart?" and shot an arrow right into my thigh.

'At the same time, my young standard bearer Raymond who was with me, was shot in the foot. He lifted his visor to see the wound and was shot between the eyes. He died instantly.

'I managed to drag myself back behind the ridge that ran between the two ditches and tried to direct the filling of the second ditch from there. The water was too deep and not enough men took part. I was very angry at the lack of men attacking but found later that the captains had disagreed on whether or not an attack was wise and some had held their men back. I received a number of messages to leave my position and get out but I ignored them. Eventually, a number of men came to me and carried me away. They put me on a horse and I was taken back to our camp at La Chapelle.

'My wound was painful but next morning I got up early and went to d'Alençon and asked him to have the trumpets sounded for another attack on Paris. He would have given the order but a number of the other captains disagreed with the move and, while they were arguing, messages came from the King ordering d'Alençon and myself to make no further attacks on the city but to report to him. We had to obey but we thought we could attack the city from another side on the way back to the King. D'Alençon had earlier had a bridge constructed over the river at St Denis and we thought if we took the troops across that bridge we could attack at a different point. When we reached the bridge, we found that our King, our Charles, had ordered the bridge to be secretly destroyed during the night and we could not cross over.'

'You mean your own king sabotaged you.'

Joan bowed her head again and bit her lip. There were tears under her eyelids. I couldn't help thinking this young woman had quite a bit to shed tears over. She had risked everything and in return had been treated with ingratitude, deceit and death.

Finally she continued and, still loyal to the King, she made no comment on his behaviour. 'We reported to the King as ordered and four days later he left Saint Denis. I was ordered to go with him. He returned to Gien and the army was disbanded for lack of funds. My beautiful duke, d'Alençon, returned to his wife. I had promised her I would send him home safe and I did. We never met again.'

'You were very fond of him.'

'Yes, probably more than anyone other than my family. I loved him as a true and loyal friend and as a courageous comrade-in-arms whom I would trust with my life. He was always there for me. A short time after the King disbanded the army and sent the captains and commanders home, d'Alençon tried to have me join him and his men on an expedition to Normandy. He asked the King to let me go but La Trémoille, and other advisors such as Regnault and Gaucourt, were determined that we should be kept apart and they advised the King against it.'

'Why did they want to keep you apart?'

'We were successful, we were popular and we usually won any battle we fought together. There were intrigues going on at the King's court that I can only guess at. The King wanted no more fighting to interrupt or jeopardize his dealings with the Duke of Burgundy. He wanted to stay safely at court and conduct diplomatic negotiations from a distance.'

'Well what was there left for you to do?'

'I spent some weeks doing very little. We went to Bourges and I stayed with Margeurite La Touroulde and her husband for three weeks. Margeurite and I got on very well together. At one time, while I was there, some of the ladies of Bourges brought me their rosary beads and asked me to touch them as a blessing.

'I said "Touch them yourself; they will benefit from your touch quite as much as from mine."

'After that, the King dragged the court to Montargis, Loches, Jargeau, Issoudun and Meung-sur-Yèvre and I was required to accompany him.

'The King's advisers recommended that we should recover the town of La Charité but that first of all we needed to take the town of Saint-Pierre-les-Moutiers.'

'But the King had disbanded the army.'

# Chapter 33: Not like the Good Old Days

'It was mainly La Trémoille who suggested attacking the town of La Charité, partly I now believe to keep me busy and out of the way. But there was another factor too. The captain in control of La Charité was a man called Perrinet Gressart. He had captured La Trémoille in 1425 and forced him to pay a large ransom as well as provide gifts to his wife and her friends. La Trémoille was determined to get even with the man.

'This was the first time I was officially given command. It was to be jointly with Charles d'Albret, La Trémoille's half-brother. We returned to Bourges to assemble an army. We needed various towns to contribute money and supplies and I wrote to several of them requesting their help. Charles never had any money so it was necessary to get support elsewhere. Orléans was very generous with money and cloth. Clermont Ferrand sent munitions and Riom provided saltpeter, sulphur and cross-bows. We set up a siege of the town of Saint-Pierre les-Moutiers for some time and on 2 November 1429 we were ordered to attack it. There were many soldiers defending the town and many of the French soldiers retreated. I was left with just four or five men who had not retreated.

'I remember good brave Jean d'Aulon, my squire. He had been badly wounded in the foot and could not walk without crutches but he saw I was almost alone in the attack and he grabbed a horse and rode out to me. He was so concerned for my safety. I remember I took my helmet off and assured him that I had 50,000 men in my company and I would not leave until I had taken the town. He told me I should retreat like the rest but I shouted out "Bring wood everybody and we'll make a bridge." The men rallied, made a bridge and we took the town. The soldiers under our command were mainly foreign mercenaries and they immediately began to plunder the church. Fortunately, I was able to stop them.

'A week later, we were preparing to attack La Cha-rité. By now, winter was setting in. We were cold, hungry, the men were unpaid and the King sent no food, money, or help. After one month of this, we were forced to give up and the town remained in Gressart's hands.

'I was back at Jargeau for Christmas and virtually unemployed.'

'This really was the beginning of the end for you wasn't it?'

'Yes, that's true. On December 29, the King con-ferred a patent of nobility upon me, my brothers, my mother and father and all their descendants. My brothers chose to use the title given to them – du Lys – but I continued to use the title "The Maid".

'I re-visited Orléans in January. That city always welcomed me and this was no exception. They gave me gifts for myself and my brother Pierre.

'I stayed with the court for most of the time and finally I was sent to join a small force under the command of a French captain called Baretta, a Scotsman called Kennedy and, the only one I knew, Ambroise de Loré.'

'Just a minute. What's a Scotsman doing there?'

Joan laughed.

'I'm sure you know the Scots and the English were enemies. Scotland and France were allies in this and other wars. Remember, it was a Scotsman who made my banners for me.

'It wasn't like old times. Alençon wasn't there. Neither was La Hire or the Bastard. But at first it seemed that the old enthusiasm and victories were returning. The town of Melun which had been in the hands of the English for ten years, had been given to the Duke of Burgundy in the previous October. The townspeople suddenly rose up and threw out the Burgundians.

'We entered Melun and it was here that I received the news that I would be captured. I was standing on the ramparts of the walled city when my Voices gave me the first warning of my capture. They repeated the message daily after that. They said I should not be surprised by it and that I should just take everything as it came and God would help me. I begged them for more details. When would it happen? They refused to tell me and repeated that I should accept it and take it well. I begged them to let me die when I was captured rather than spend time in prison. They did not reply.

'It was to be a whole month of waiting and wondering before their prediction came true.'

# Chapter 34: Not the Done Thing

'Joan, I haven't tried to understand the origin of your voices. You believed in them and I confess I'm more interested in what you did as a result of that faith. You accomplished amazing things for a peasant, a female and a teenager.'

'Yes. I had faith. There are many people who have heard voices and their stories have also been documented. I can't explain it but those voices gave me the courage and the strength to do the things I did.

'From Melun, I went back to Lagny with Kennedy, Baretta and Ambroise de Loré's lieutenant. We had a minor success against a small English marauding party there. The group was led by a man called Franquet d'Arras. He had been in the service of the previous Duke of Burgundy as early as 1416 and had been on a marauding expedition into France with about three hundred men. I decided to put an end to his plundering. With help from the garrison at Lagny, we were able to defeat his band and capture Franquet himself.

'I decided I would hold him for ransom and exchange him for a Parisian, Jacquet Guillaume who had been imprisoned for an attempted plot to let the French into Paris to drive the Burgundians out. I then learnt that Guillaume had been executed. I would have set Franquet free but the bailiffs told me this would be a great wrong and that he should be punished for the many crimes he had committed. I handed him over to them and I remember I said "Because my man is dead whom I wished to save, do with him what you ought to do in justice." His crimes were so extensive as a murderer and thief that his trial lasted fifteen days. He was found guilty and beheaded.'

'His death led to many people condemning your actions, didn't it? Why was that if he was guilty of so many crimes?'

'In the eyes of military men, I had broken the code of war. They thought of Franquet as a brave man and a good fighter who had been captured for ransom. In their opinion, I should have not submitted him to a civil trial.'

'What was the other incident at Lagny that your own trial judges used against you?'

'There was a baby that had supposedly been still-born. The girls of the town went to pray for the child in front of a statue of the Virgin Mary and they asked me to join them. We prayed for some time when the child suddenly yawned three times. It was taken to be baptized but it died not long after. It was then able to be buried in consecrated ground. People believed that I had brought the baby back to life. It was a superstitious age but, I have to say, even now, people believe strange things, particularly if they want badly enough to believe them.'

'It was at Lagny that you changed swords, wasn't it?'

'Yes, my beautiful sword from Fierbois was broken and I carried a good sword taken from a Burgundian after that.'

'How did the sword break?'

Joan looked a bit embarrassed at this question and, for a moment, I thought she would not answer. Finally she spoke. 'I broke it on the backside of a prostitute.'

'What?'

'Yes. I would not allow these women to travel with the army, corrupting the soldiers. I drove them away at every opportunity. I believed we were doing God's work and we should keep ourselves in God's grace. I chased this woman away and, since I had nothing else available, I whacked her rump with the flat of my sword.'

'Not particularly saintly behaviour. Let's move on.'

Joan managed a smile at that. 'I never did consider myself a saint. Or for that matter anyone particularly special.'

She paused to regain the thread of her story then continued. 'My voices had told me I had only one year at the most to perform my mission and I knew that time was running out. Charles was continuing his negotiations with the Duke of Burgundy mostly behind my back. It was becoming obvious even to Charles that the English and the Burgundians had no intention of reaching a fair agreement with him. In fact on 23 April 1430, the young English king, Henry VI, landed at Calais with an army to join up with the Burgundians and the English already here.

'In those days, the position of bridges across the many rivers was vital to the movement of armies. To defend and maintain Paris, the English and the Burgundians were on the wrong side of the various rivers. The most strategic town at the time was Compiègne which was loyal to Charles, so loyal you remember they refused to let him give them away to the Duke of Burgundy as a bargaining piece. To get to Paris, it was necessary to go through Compiègne. The English and the Burgundians began to draw up their armies towards Compiègne.'

I asked gently, 'Compiègne was where you spent your last days of freedom, wasn't it?'

Joan looked away briefly. 'Yes,' she said. 'I'll meet you there and tell you more then. *Au revoir.*' And she was gone.

# SECTION 9: COMPIEGNE

# Chapter 35: Compiègne under Attack

Compiègne is less than an hour by train from Paris. It pays tribute to Joan's life with a statue in the main square. However, this town became better known in the twentieth century for the signing of the armistice to end World War 1. The famous peace treaty was signed at the eleventh hour of the eleventh day of the eleventh month, 1918 with the surrender of the Germans. Hitler had sweet revenge in 1940 when he forced the French to surrender in exactly the same spot in 1940 during the early days of World War 2. The French World War 1 memorial was destroyed by the Germans but was restored to its pre-1940 state in 1950.

I headed towards the cathedral assuming Joan would meet me there. Almost three hundred years after Joan's time, the cathedral in Compiègne had a considerable upgrade during the reign of Louis XIV, the Sun King. His wife, the empress liked to spend time at the Compiègne castle, and the plain interior of the cathedral was given a facelift with wood, gold, marble and crystal throughout to suit her more expensive tastes.

Sitting at the back of the church, I waited. I did not wait long.

'*Bonjour encore*,' said a soft feminine voice. Her contemporaries had commented on the soft feminine nature of her voice though she was quite capable of giving anyone of them a tongue lashing.

'*Bonjour*, Joan,' I replied. 'Tell me about your time here in Compiègne.'

Without hesitation, she took up the story. 'I went to Compiègne on 13 May 1430. There I was housed with a royal official and his household. I slept with his wife as was the custom in those days mainly to protect women from rape or unwanted sexual advances during the night. I remember waking her up several times during the night to go and warn her husband against the treason of the Burgundians. I felt very distressed as though danger was very close.

'The next morning, I went to Mass very early, confessed and took Communion. I always did that before I went into battle. The townspeople, particularly the children crowded into the church to see me. I was standing beside a pillar when I was overcome with such a sense of danger that I called out to them:

"My children and dear friends, I tell you that I have been sold and betrayed, and that soon I shall be delivered to death. So I beg you to pray God for me, for I will no longer have any power to serve the king, or the Kingdom of France."

'If you look at a map of the area in those days, what I am going to tell you now will make more sense.'

I gave her a blank page from my notebook and a spare pen from my bag. This time she took the pen as though ballpoints were standard issue in her army and then drew a clear map.

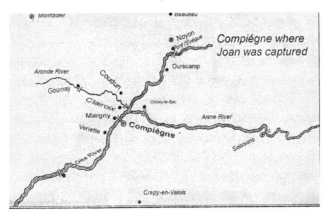

Compiègne where Joan was captured

'As I told you, bridges were vital to victory and this time was no exception.

'The Duke of Burgundy had arrived with his army at Noyon. See it here at the top of the map, north of Compiègne. It was reasonable to suppose that he would cross the River Oise here at the bridge of Pont l'Evêque which was held by his allies, the English. From there he could attack at Choisy-le-Bac, take the bridge there and attack Compiègne.

'I was determined to stop him. With my old comrade Poton de Saintrailles, and a small army we headed to Pont l' Evêque. The English held the bridge bravely and when the garrison from Noyon arrived to help them, we were forced to retreat in to Compiègne.

'Two days later the people at Choisy-le-Bac surrendered to the Duke of Burgundy. This meant that the only bridge I could use to get troops across the river to get at the Burgundians from behind was twenty miles to the east at Soissons. So I led the army to Soissons.

'I was accompanied by my good friend the Count of Vendôme. It was he who introduced me to the

181

Dauphin at Chinon. That seemed like a lifetime away. It was also he who rejoiced with me when Charles' scheme of retiring to the Loire valley after his coronation was prevented and we stayed to fight the English.

'I was also accompanied by the Archbishop of Reims. He was always very flattering to my face but I learned later that he went against me in secret at every opportunity. Our army arrived at Soissons in the evening and to my shock, we were refused entrance. The captain, Guichard Bournel (a Picard and the Picards were fighting on the side of the English) refused us entry on the grounds that such an army would cause havoc if it were allowed to enter the town. Only I, Vendôme, the Archbishop and a few attendants were allowed to spend the night in the town. The rest of the army was forced to sleep in the fields.

'It turned out later that Bournel was planning to sell the town of Soissons to the Duke of Burgundy and he did this a few weeks later for 4,000 *saluts d'or* [8]payment. I have to say, I was furious and I did say at the time that if I could get hold of him, I would cut him into four pieces.'

'I can understand that. So what were you to do next?'

'Now we had a dilemma on our hands. There was not enough food in Compiègne to feed the army so there was no use taking them back there. We were forced to disband and go our separate ways. I was left with Baretta and about two to three hundred men.

---

[8] Probably worth about 1.25 livres-tournois per salut d'or at the time.

'But it got worse. While I was away, the Burgundians laid siege to Compiègne. They set up three encampments on the opposite side of the River Oise from Compiègne. If you look at that map again, I'll explain the set up. Just one kilometer from the town, at Margny, the Picards set up camp under the leadership of Baudot de Noyelles; two kilometers away at Venette, the English lead by Sir John Montgomery set up their camp and four kilometers away at Clairoix, Jean of Luxembourg was camped with his Burgundians and Flemings. The Duke of Burgundy was stationed at Coudun by then. All in all, about 6,000 men.

# Chapter 36: Caught!

'I was determined to help in the defense of the town. Some of my men thought it too risky with so few of us but I managed to persuade them and, at midnight on 22 May, we set out for Compiègne. There was no moon and we had to ride very carefully watching out for Burgundians and rabbit holes. We arrived at the town around 4 a.m. and entered on the far side away from the enemy.

'Having ridden most of the night, we rested till around 5 p.m. that afternoon then I decided it was time to take the offensive and attack the closest group at Margny. I led a band of about five hundred men across the bridge and into the enemy camp. We took them by surprise and would have defeated them easily but I did not know that this was to be the moment my time had run out.

'By a stroke of very bad luck, Jean of Luxembourg happened to be on his way to visit the camp at Margny to discuss strategy with Baudot de Noyelles. From a hill, he saw what I was doing and sent word for his own troops to come to the rescue. Troops joined the battle from Venette and Clairoix and even from Coudun. We were hopelessly outnumbered and forced to retreat. I remained at the rear to cover the withdrawal.'

I interrupted her with 'I have read that even the Burgundians spoke of your courageous fight at the rear of your troops protecting them as they withdrew into the town.'

Joan was silent for a while then went on.

'As the enemy troops were right on top of us, the decision was made in the town to raise the drawbridge. Most of our troops had made it back to safety. As the drawbridge went up, those of us defending the rear were left outside the gate. Some of the soldiers who had been on the drawbridge when it was raised, were thrown into the river. Several of them drowned but the Burgundians took pity on others and held out their lances to pull them from the river.

'We were trapped outside. My brother Pierre was with me as was my faithful squire d'Aulon and his brother Poton and a few others. We kept fighting and I managed to urge my horse away from the gate and into the meadow. Strange the things you remember at times of high danger. I remember the horse, a beautiful dapple grey, very fiery. I was surrounded and arms and hands were reaching out to grab me, grab the horse, voices shouting "Yield to me!" Everyone wanted to be the one to capture The Maid. Finally it was a Picard archer who got hold of my surcoat and pulled me off the horse. I was then taken prisoner by Guillaume de Wendonne, a man-at-arms serving under Jean of Luxembourg and in command of a company. I and my friends were prisoners.'

Joan and I sat in the cathedral in Compiègne in silence. No matter how many times I had read Joan's story, this was always one of the saddest moments for me. I thought about the things I had read while Joan sat beside me and said nothing. In this day and age of Hollywood endings, we would expect the townspeople and soldiers in the town to stream out to the rescue of their heroine. They did not. Common sense prevailed. The good of the many outweighed the rescue of the few.

Joan's capture caused tremendous joy among the English and the Burgundians. There was a not-so-small problem however. Whose prisoner was she?

A Picard archer had captured her. He was under the command of Guillaume Wendonne who was himself under the command of Jean of Luxembourg. Jean of Luxembourg served the Duke of Burgundy and through him the King of England. Each of them had a claim on the eighteen-year old prisoner.

The protocol of chivalry and war at the time was that such a high status prisoner would be held in physical safety even comfort while a process of bargaining over ransom took place. Such a prisoner was worth a great deal of money or could be used as an exchange for other important prisoners on the opposite side.

None of this customary protocol was offered to Joan of Arc although the reign of chivalry was at its height, and women were supposed to be protected by every knight whose duty it was to help them. As a prisoner of war and as a woman, Joan was not treated in any way that was customary. The English were so outraged at being beaten by a woman that they concluded she could not be an ordinary woman and her power must come from the Devil. In other words, she was a witch. But there was another more potent enemy waiting to pounce on the captive Maid.

The Catholic Church intended to try her as a heretic. She claimed to be given direct instructions from God which meant she bypassed their authority. The churchmen and only the churchmen had the right to interpret God's instructions. In their view, this upstart of a woman was putting herself above them and providing an example to others which was a danger to their authority. She must be made an example of.

# Chapter 37: The Long Arm of Mother Church

The Church acted quickly. As soon as news of her capture was known in Paris, the Vicar General of the Inquisition sent a letter to the Duke of Burgundy demanding that she be handed over to the church.

Letters were sent to Jean of Luxembourg by the University of Paris, demanding that she be handed over to them to be tried for "idolatry and other matters". The University of Paris was a church institute not a university as we understand the term today. It consisted of the most eminent churchmen and had the highest authority. When Joan's Herald, Guienne, was imprisoned by the English at Orléans, they sent off to the University of Paris to get permission to burn him.

Sitting beside me, Joan remained silent and I considered the politics surrounding her at the time of her capture.

The man of the moment in the scramble for possession of Joan was Pierre Cauchon, the Bishop of Beauvais. He had been Rector of the University of Paris and played a leading role at the time the University took the side of the Burgundians against the Armagnacs (Joan's side), upholding the theory of the double monarchy that the King of England was also King of France. Cauchon had been one of the negotiators at the Treaty of Troyes which had disinherited the Dauphin.

In August 1420 he had been elected Bishop of Beauvais. He enjoyed the confidence of the Duke of Bedford who was Regent of England and France and also received an income of 1,000 pounds as a member of the Council of Henry VI, the child king of England. He was highly regarded by the University of Paris and the Pope, Martin V. He had been living in Reims before the coronation of Charles VII but was forced to flee when Joan brought Charles there. He had also lost his diocese of Beauvais and was forced to leave that town when it opened its gates to Charles VII. All this, thanks to Joan. He had been forced to flee to Rouen and he consequently had no love for The Maid.

Like many on the English side, Cauchon believed that the crowning of Charles VII could be discredited if it were shown that the person behind the French victory was a heretic and a witch. He also had his eye on the archbishopric of Rouen which had recently fallen vacant and he had hopes of obtaining it for good services rendered to the English Burgundian side.

The Duke of Bedford requested Cauchon to claim Joan since she had been captured in his diocese. Cauchon visited Jean of Luxembourg with promises of payment by the English if they would hand Joan over to him. His expenses for his journeys of negotiation were paid for by the English. The University of Paris again demanded that Jean of Luxembourg hand over The Maid to Cauchon for trial by the Church. The pressure was on but Jean of Luxembourg delayed. He would not hand over his prisoner until he saw the money. The money to buy Joan was raised by a tax on the Duchy of Normandy and when it was paid, Joan was handed over to the Church in November 1430 and moved to Rouen where Pierre Cauchon was planning her trial. He told one of the notaries of the court that he intended to make "a beautiful trial of this".

Bringing myself back to the present, I broke the silence. 'Joan, did they treat you well as a prisoner and where did they take you?'

'I was treated very well while I was a prisoner of Jean of Luxembourg. It was only when the Church got hold of me that things changed. At first I was held under guard at Jean of Luxembourg's camp at Clairoux. The Duke of Burgundy came to look me over while I was there; he didn't say much. I heard later though that he was so pleased to see me captured that he wrote some very excited letters to the citizens of Saint Quentin and to the Duke of Brittany telling them the news.

'I was taken to the fortress of Beaulieu and my good and faithful d'Aulon was allowed to stay with me.'

# Chapter 38: Escape Attempts

'Is it from there that you tried to escape?' I asked.

'Yes, I was kept in one of the towers in a room with a wooden floor. I managed to pull up a couple of planks and got down into the room below. The guards did not notice and I was about to lock them in their own guard room when, again by bad luck, a porter came in and gave the alarm. I say by bad luck because he had never entered that room before. I was recaptured and put in a small dark cell.'

'Had you lost faith that your saints would help you?'

'Not at all. But I did believe that God helps those who help themselves. We have to act first and then we will receive what help we need.

'Early in June, I was moved again. This time to Jean of Luxembourg's castle of Beaurevoir near the town of Saint Quentin. I was placed in the care of three women, all called Joan. They were Jean of Luxembourg's elderly aunt, his wife and his stepdaughter. I still remember them with deep affection. Joan of Luxembourg told me she had fallen on her knees and begged her nephew not to sell me but he would not listen. The three of them tried to get me to wear female clothes too and offered to bring me a dress or the cloth to make one. I refused.'

'While you were at Beaurevoir, a Burgundian knight, Haimond de Macy, visited and spoke with you several times.'

'Yes, he was a good fellow. Harmless enough and he would try to touch my breasts in a teasing way but I pushed him away every time.'

'Yes, he gave evidence at your rehabilitation trial and mentioned that. He said you were "of decent conduct both in speech and act". It's there in Beaurevoir that you made another escape attempt, wasn't it?'

'Yes. I was worried, very worried about the good, loyal citizens of Compiègne. I had heard that the English plan was to put everyone over the age of seven to fire or sword when the town was captured. I was also aware that I was being sold to the English and I absolutely dreaded that. On top of all that, I had heard that my Dauphin, Charles VII, King of France, was doing nothing to help me, neither rescue nor ransom. I would rather have died than be sold to the English. I was depressed and desperate. I decided to escape.

'My voices told me not to do it but I was determined. St Catherine told me almost every day that I must not leap and that God would help me and also help the people of Compiègne. I said to St Catherine that since God would help the people of Compiègne, I myself would like to be there. So, sometime in August, while I was allowed to walk on the top of the tower, I commended myself to God and jumped.'

She paused a moment and I added what I knew of the event. 'It's been estimated that the tower was sixty or seventy feet high. That's between 18 and 21 metres. You should have been killed but all that happened was you were knocked unconscious and seem to have suffered from concussion.'

'When they found me, I was unconscious and even when I returned to consciousness, I was very dazed and I was in pain for some days. I couldn't eat for two or three days after that but then my voices told me to ask God's forgiveness and that the people of Compiègne would be relieved before Martinmas which was 11 November. I was able to eat after that and recovered.'

'Was Compiègne saved before Martinmas?'I asked.

'Yes, it was,' she replied.

'In this case, you deliberately disobeyed your voices. This would seem to rule out the explanation that your voices said only what you wanted them to say or that they were the outward expression of your own inner desires.'

'I don't have the answer for you. As I said before, I was not the first one to hear voices or to successfully foretell the future. And there have been others before and since. Probably more than we realize because if you're going to be thought mad or a heretic, it's not a thing everyone would tell others about.'

I nodded. 'That leap from the tower was miraculous too. You should have been killed or at least badly injured. That's caused a lot of theories to fly round as people have tried to explain it. Some speculated that you climbed through a lower window or that you made a rope of bedclothes and let yourself down as far as possible but we know from the evidence at your trial that this is not the case.'

'Again I don't know why I wasn't killed. I wish I had died at that time but it didn't happen.

'After that, I was moved to Arras and kept in the Cour le Comte, the residence of the Duke of Burgundy, in the centre of the city. The Duke was holding court there at the time but he did not visit me. I was visited by a number of other people though. Two men from Tournai came and brought me money to buy necessities. I was very grateful for that as I had nothing but the clothes I was captured in, minus the armour of course. Another visitor was Jean de Pressy, councilor and Chamberlain to the Duke of Burgundy. He visited me several times and each time he told me to wear women's clothes..

'From Arras I was taken to the castle of Drugy near Saint-Riquier. I was visited by a group of monks and by citizens of Saint-Riquier. All of these people treated me with respect and compassion. From there I was transferred to the castle of Crotoy at the mouth of the Somme. This was the first time I had seen the sea and although my glimpse was fleeting, I was overawed by it. At Crotoy, I thought often of my friend d'Alençon. He had been imprisoned for five years in the same place by the English after the Battle of Verneuil. Fortunately he knew he would be ransomed and that it was just a matter of time. I had no such salvation ahead of me.

'While I was at Crotoy, the ladies of Abbeville took a boat down the river and came to visit me. I enjoyed their visit very much and asked them to remember me in their prayers and kissed them as they left.'

I commented: 'It's said they considered you a marvel of their sex.'

'I don't know about that but I was so moved by them that I declared I would wish to be buried in their country.

'A fellow prisoner was Nicolas de Queuville, Chancellor of the Cathedral of Amiens. He had been among those who plotted to hand over the town of Amiens to Charles. Two of his accomplices had been executed and he was lucky to escape with his life. He was allowed to celebrate mass in the prison and I attended and made my confession to him.

'Finally, the day arrived when negotiations were completed, the money had been paid to Jean of Luxembourg and I was handed over to the tender mercy of the Church. On 20 December 1430, I was taken across the mouth of the River Somme by boat to Saint Valery and on to Eu where I was kept in the prison of the castle there. From there, I was moved to Dieppe and arrived in Rouen towards the end of December, not long after Christmas.'

'By then you had been a prisoner for seven months.'

'Yes, a prisoner of Jean of Luxembourg. Things were about to change. Although I was supposed to be in the arms of Mother Church, I was in the hands of the English. I was in a secular prison not an ecclesiastical one. By rights, as someone about to be tried by the Church, I should have been held in the Archbishopric prison and guarded by women. Time to move on. I'll see you in Rouen.'

And she was gone.

# SECTION 10: ROUEN

# Chapter 39: Feel the Heat!

I was concerned about the visit to Rouen. How would Joan feel or react to this town where she had suffered and died so horribly?

I took the train from Paris to Rouen. Apart from its infamous place in the story of Joan of Arc, Rouen has a great deal of its medieval buildings still intact but badly scarred. Many are chipped and damaged by the impact of bullets during the battles of World War 2. An amazing contrast of architectural beauty and ugly destruction.

The streets, the houses, the churches and the old town clock are delightful remnants of the past. I almost expected a Pied Piper to come dancing along with laughing children following him through the streets. Only the modern clothing of the many tourists kept me anchored in the present.

The beautiful cathedral was worth the visit. On display were photos of the bomb damage to the building in 1944. It has been totally restored now and must be one of the loveliest of its style.

The June day was incredibly hot. At first, I could not bring myself to enter the market place to look at the spot where Joan had been burnt alive, her charred, naked body displayed to the crowd to prove that she was a woman. So many could not believe a woman had done the amazing things that she had. Then they raked the coals around her again and let the fire finish its work. All but her heart was totally burnt – or so the legend says.

I visited the Joan of Arc museum and then the tower of Rouen where Joan was imprisoned. Only one tower still stands but originally there had been four of them.

*The remaining tower in Rouen where Joan was held prisoner during her trial.*

Finally I walked to the market place, crossed the square and looked at the tall pole that marks the position of the stake. Beside it now is a beautiful and very modern church – l'Eglise Sainte-Jeanne d'Arc (the church of Joan of Arc). It is one of the most beautiful churches I have ever seen. Small, with two sides totally made of stained glass, it is not in the traditional shape of a church but consists of a series of angles, straight lines and curves. Inside, the simplicity of polished wood reflects the light streaming through the stained glass walls. Strangely, unlike other churches I'd seen, it did not depict the story of Joan of Arc. The only mention of her was in its name.

I walked out into the sunshine again and the heat hit me like the opening of an oven door. Crossing the square, I climbed a few steps and sat down at one of the shaded outdoor tables of a tavern overlooking the square. When the waiter arrived, I ordered an ice cold beer.

Once again Joan joined me.

'Good morning, Joan. Are you ready to continue?'

'Yes – but what would you like to talk about today?'

'Tell me again about wearing men's clothing. It's the one thing they finally used to justify burning you, when all else failed.'

'It's not simple and the reason changed over time. It began as a disguise to get about safely in a time of war. A young woman didn't just go traipsing round the countryside in those days. To use a well-worn accusation, that would have been "just asking for it."

*The place where Joan was burned.*
*Behind it is the Church of Joan of Arc.*
*To the right is a statue of Joan against the wall of the*
*church.*

'Yes, I can understand that. Rape is a common phenomenon in war. Always has been. Still is.'

'There was also the convenience of getting around. Not just riding a horse but just walking. Have you seen what women wore in those days? Great dragging skirts, soon covered in mud. We didn't have hard footpaths or even boardwalks. Just dirt or, more often, mud.

'The freedom I felt just walking around in men's clothing, was a real eye opener. I now think women were and are crazy to put up with the constraints of conventional feminine clothing. It actually makes you feel constrained and always vulnerable. I've taken an interest in women's fashion ever since.'

'Really! That's not a side of you many of your admirers, or detractors, would suspect. Although you were known to enjoy beautiful clothes during your mission, they were always male clothes. You were wearing a beautiful golden cloak when you were captured.'

'Well, I'm speaking politically more than fashionably. Women's clothes in many cultures are restrictive. Think of high heel shoes (not to mention foot binding), and corsets and long skirts that get in the way particularly when they later put hoops in them. A woman is very vulnerable in a skirt. That was my horrible experience when I was imprisoned here in Rouen. My leggings, tightly laced were my only protection against the English soldiers who stayed in my cell with me the entire time. Just think about it. Male dress was the one thing they used to condemn me when all their fine convoluted arguments failed. Why was it so important? The fact that it sealed my death sentence made a lasting impression on me. Why wouldn't I be interested in the topic. I get quite heated over it – no pun intended.'

We were sitting overlooking the town square. Rouen was baking in the heat. I looked at Joan but her eyes were fixed on the tall staff in the square, the staff that marked the place where once a stake stood high, so high, the executioner wept because he could not reach the victim to end her life mercifully by strangulation as was the custom.

In spite of the heat, I shivered. Joan put her face in her hands and her whole body shuddered. I began to think that meeting her here had been a mistake.

I broke the silence. 'Joan, would you like to go somewhere else?'

She didn't reply immediately but I waited. Finally she spoke.

'No. I think I will be all right in a minute. I've had centuries to get over this but burning to death is not easily forgotten. If I had known how it would all end I don't think I would ever have left my father and mother's house. Mercifully, I didn't know until the very last day. I always believed I would be protected or rescued or that I would escape. I never thought it could happen. It would have been too horrible to imagine and I don't think I could have gone on as I did.'

'Joan. I'm so sorry. I don't know what to say. Please, let's go somewhere else and sit for a while.'

Joan stood up without a word. We walked down the steps into the square. As we passed the tall white staff with the cross on top, Joan turned her face away and quickened her pace. We passed the beautiful little church that bears her name and mingled with the crowd of tourists ambling through the medieval streets. I realised that none of them could see her.

I wondered if Joan recognised any of the town but she had spent most of her time here locked in a tower or standing in chains in front of dozens of hostile men determined to murder her legally.

I looked at the cheerful faces of the passing tourists, holiday makers admiring the architecture, buying their souvenirs. It was clear that Joan was very uncomfortable in this town of her trial and death. Still, it had played a major role in her story and it was obvious we had to include it and those dreadful events.

Joan looked at the ancient buildings and shook her head sadly at the bullet marks on the beautiful old stonework.

'You're much more destructive in every way than we were, you know. Your technological developments are a two-edged sword.' She smiled at the expression. 'But who'd use a sword these days?'

We came to the one remaining tower of the building where she'd spent the last months of her nineteen years of life. She gazed up at the windows high above the ground.

'I'd like to talk about your captivity and trial another time. Let's go visit the cathedral. We can sit there for a while and just absorb its peace and calm. Personally, I feel exhausted and horrified just talking to you about these things. I can't begin to imagine how you felt or still feel.'

Joan nodded and we walked to the cathedral. In the cool interior, we sat as far from the wandering tourists as possible. I noticed Joan did not acknowledge the altar or bow her head or show any signs of the deep religious fervour she was so well known for. Her eyes were wide open and her jaw set tight.

There was no sign of the good humoured young woman of our earlier interviews. Visiting this town had obviously revived long-buried memories of the horror of what had been done to her. I suggested we pick up our story at another time, in another place.

Joan gave me a grateful smile, nodded, stood up and was gone.

# Chapter 40: Chained like an Animal

I let out a long sigh. I felt I had been holding my breath for an hour. It was then I decided not to interview Joan about the last months of her life. Most of what happened to her once she arrived in Rouen as the property of the English, is far too painful for me to ask her to recall and comment on. I decided to draw on the extensive records of the time for much of it and return to interviewing Joan when it seemed appropriate.

Joan was imprisoned in the second largest tower of the castle at Rouen, facing the fields. She was not in a dungeon below ground, but she was in a room in the center of the tower, with no windows. The room she was kept in was up a flight of eight stairs. The child King of England, Henry VI and his court were also staying in the castle for part of the time but Joan did not see him.

Her cell contained no furniture although she was given a bed of some sort when she became ill.

She was in leg irons and chained to a block of wood. At night an additional chain was placed around her waist and chained to the wall. The English were determined she would not escape and she refused to give any promises that she would not try. At one stage, they had a cage made especially for her. It was designed to hold a prisoner standing upright with neck, arms and legs held tight. Fortunately, it was never used on Joan.

Her guards were five rough English soldiers who took delight in harassing her day and night, taunting her and even attempting to rape her. Three of them were in the cell with her and two were outside the door. At one time, she was only saved from rape by the unexpected appearance of the Earl of Warwick who had heard her shouts for help.

She had no privacy for dressing or calls of nature and no peace from her guards. They delighted in waking her up at night and telling her she had been condemned and was to be executed immediately. She complained to Cauchon and to the Earl of Warwick that she did not dare to remove her leggings or to wear them unless they were tightly laced, since her guards had tried to do violence to her. Warwick changed some members of the guard but this did not change the continued sadistic taunting and harassment.

A tailor was commissioned to make her a dress. He came to her cell to take her measurements and, while doing so, took the opportunity to fondle her breasts. She gave him a whack across the ear that sent him flying.

There was also a room beside her cell with a spy hole through which others could watch and listen to her without her knowing they were there. This was put to good use as we shall see later.

Joan's virginity had always been an important aspect of her acceptance as pure and not a tool of the Devil. While the Duke of Bedford was visiting Rouen from 1 to 13 January 1431, his wife, Anne of Burgundy, and some other ladies of the court were requested to examine Joan. They did this in her cell and declared her to be a virgin intact. The Duke of Bedford hid in the room beside Joan's cell and watched the examination in secret through the spy hole. This evidence of her virginity which would have been in her favour, was never mentioned at her trial.

During this time, on 6 January, Joan turned nineteen. It would be her last birthday.

As we have seen, Pierre Cauchon, the Bishop of Beauvais, was put in charge of the trial and he intended to make it "a beautiful trial" indeed. He received a letter from the English on 3 January, formally handing Joan over to him. This was merely a formality as Joan was not taken to a Church prison where she would have been guarded by women but remained in her prison cell guarded by English soldiers.

Before the inquisitorial trial could go ahead, evidence of prior evil doing and bad reputation had to be produced. Cauchon sent numerous agents to the many places Joan had been -- including her childhood home of Domremy. Their job was to collect information on her past behaviour.

Each one failed to provide the information Cauchon needed. Some were sent back to try again but could find nothing and were accused of being traitors. Another who investigated Joan's past and reported back to Cauchon was told he was a traitor and a bad man and his expenses were not paid because he had produced nothing useful. He later commented that he had found nothing about Joan which he would not have liked to find about his own sister.

Although no evidence of evil doing could be found the trial went ahead anyway but none of these good findings was included in the evidence produced during the trial. Initially, ten sittings of the trial were conducted between 9 January and 20 February 1431. Joan was not present at these sessions. She remained in her cell and her chains.

At one time, Jean of Luxembourg came to see her in her prison. It was he who had first held Joan prisoner and had finally sold her to the English for six thousand francs although his own aunt had gone down on her knees and begged him not to do it.

He entered Joan's cell accompanied by the Bishop of Thérouenne and the English Earls of Warwick and Stafford. He told Joan that he would ransom her if she would promise never to take arms again. Joan saw through his cruel lie. She was no longer his to ransom. He had sold her to the English, accepted their money and they would never let her go.

Standing defiantly in chains, Joan told him she knew the English were going to kill her in the belief that they would regain the Kingdom of France.

'But,' she said 'even if they were a hundred thousand Godons more than they are now, they should not have the kingdom.'

The Earl of Stafford was so angry that he drew his dagger and tried to stab her but the Earl of Warwick stopped him. Not out of pity or decency. He had a crueller death in mind for Joan.

# Chapter 41: A Presumptuous Woman

The English always intended to burn Joan. The trial was a sham to legitimize the burning. Many were convinced she was a witch. How else could she have defeated their previously invincible armies? The fact that she was female made matters worse. Not many men can take being beaten by a girl. Their pride was stung. They wanted to erase the shame and make her pay.

But as I mentioned before, Joan's behavior was a serious affront and a threat to an even more powerful institution, the Catholic Church. Joan's belief in her direct contact with her saints and through them, with God, went against the power structure and teachings of the Church. As we have seen, only the Churchmen could define God's will and everyone else came to God through the Churchmen. Joan's claim for a direct line of communication was an affront and a threat to the power of the clergy. As Churchmen, her judges and assessors were accustomed to the devotion and obedience of women. To them, Joan was an independent and presumptuous woman who took private instructions through her saints rather than through any priest. This could not be tolerated. There were very few of her accusers who were not affected by this sense of outrage. They too would punish her for her presumption. From this perspective, some writers have called her the first Protestant martyr.

During the trial, Joan was never told what she was accused of. She was not given a defence advocate. She had to conduct her own defence against unknown charges. Not a single witness was called on her behalf. She was alone, unable to even read or check the documents prepared for her signature. Any who tried to advise or encourage her were threatened with dismissal, imprisonment or worse.

Jean de la Fontaine was suspected of giving Joan some advice which might have helped her to defeat the judges' intentions. He was forced to leave Rouen in a hurry. André Marguerie who asked a question considered unhelpful in convicting Joan, was told to hold his tongue. Nicholas de Houppeville was thrown into prison for voicing a criticism of the trial. Isambard de la Pierre attempted to advise Joan and was told to "be silent in the Devil's name". Jean Lefèvre remarked during the trial that a particular question put to Joan was "a big question" and that she was not bound to answer it. In spite of his status as a bishop, he too was told to be silent.

The trial began on the basis of a charge of witchcraft but shifted to heresy during the proceedings. Heresy was an intellectual crime, a way of thinking, and it was very difficult to prove one's innocence once charged. In such a trial, facts were of less importance than knowing what was in the heart and mind of the accused. The principal aim of interrogation was to get the accused to confess. Confession then lead to condemnation. Torture was the common means of obtaining a confession. Burning was the usual method of death.

The two judges were Cauchon and Jean Lemaistre, Dominican Vicar in Rouen, Vice Inquisitor of France. He proved most reluctant to take part at all and tried to get out of it. The Inquisitor however was taking part in another trial and Lemaistre, as Vice Inquisitor, was forced to fill in for him.

Apart from the two judges, there were close to one hundred assessors. The assembly of learned men who confronted Joan consisted of one cardinal, six bishops, thirty-two doctors of theology, seven doctors of medicine and one hundred and three other associates. They were French churchmen who were loyal to the Duke of Burgundy or supporters of the English. They were all French with the exception of two relatively uninfluential Englishmen at the trial. The assessors were mostly from the University of Paris and most were considered to be among the best ecclesiastical minds of the time. They were all regarded as of the highest character and intellect.

This massive gathering was brought together to interrogate an uneducated country girl of nineteen years of age. They did not all attend the trial all of the time so that each day of the trial saw a different cross section of them asking Joan questions that in many cases had been asked and answered on other days.

When the trial began, Joan had been a prisoner for eight months, the last two of which she had spent chained in a cell in Rouen. She remained in chains throughout the trial.

*Joan on trial.*

# Chapter 42: Let's Try a Little Treachery

Before the trial began, Cauchon directed one of the trial assessors, Nicolas Loiselleur, to trick Joan and to gain her confidence. Loiselleur was a priest, had been a canon of Rouen since 1421, and was a personal friend of Cauchon's. He was to visit Joan in her cell, dressed not as a priest but as an ordinary citizen and to pretend to be a supporter of "her King", Charles VII. Two of the trial notaries, Guillaume Manchon and Boisguillaume, were to hide in the room next to her cell and watch and listen to the conversation.

Loiselleur visited Joan several times and the guards left him alone with her. Manchon and Boisguillaume listened through the spy hole. Desperate and alone, Joan believed Loiselleur and he drew her on to talk about her voices. Later, he revealed that he was a priest and heard her confession several times.

Cauchon later demanded that the two notaries enter what they had heard in the register of the trial but both had the courage to refuse.

On Friday, 21 February, 1431, Joan was taken to the royal chapel in the courtyard of the castle. It was here that her trial began. She was still in chains and was seated at a wooden table facing her judges and assessors.

The trouble began immediately when they demanded that Joan swear an oath to tell the truth.

Joan replied: 'I do not know what you will ask me about. Perhaps you will ask me things which I shall not tell you.'

She was making sure she could protect the things she had told the Dauphin in confidence. Finally she consented to take a very limited oath. She was then questioned about her parentage, her background and religious education.

Three or four notaries were appointed to record the proceedings. One of these, Guillaume Manchon recalled what happened.

'At the first interrogation, in the chapel in Rouen, on the occasion of the first questions put to Joan, a great tumult arose. Joan was interrupted at every word when she spoke about her apparitions; and there were two or three secretaries of the English King who recorded her declarations according to their own fantasy, omitting her excuses and all that pointed to her discharge. I complained and said that if things were not more orderly, I would not accept the responsibility of holding the pen.'

Cauchon asked Joan to repeat the *Pater Noster* (Our Father) but she refused saying that she would only if he heard her in confession. As the session concluded, Cauchon forbade Joan to leave her prison. Joan again refused to accept this, saying that, if she did manage to escape, she would not have broken her word. Finally she complained of being kept in irons and chained up. This was ignored. And the first session ended.

After the uproar of the first day, it was decided to hold the trial in the robing room behind the great hall of the castle with two English guards on the door.

Joan was taken to and from her prison by Jean Massieu who had been appointed by Cauchon. As he was taking her across the castle court yard, she asked if the Host (the wafer consecrated in Holy Communion as the body of Christ) was displayed in any accessible place. When he replied that this was done in the castle chapel, she begged him to change their route so that they would pass it. He agreed and when they reached the chapel, Joan knelt and said her prayers.

When Cauchon heard of this he was furious and ordered Massieu not to tolerate any such prayers again. The *promoter* (similar to today's prosecutor), Jean d'Estivet had developed a particular hatred for Joan. He raged at Massieu and his words are recorded. He shouted at Massieu:

> *Recreant, what made you so bold as to allow this excommunicated whore to approach the church without permission? I'll have you put in a tower where you'll see neither moon nor sun for a month, if you do anything else.*[9]

Amazingly, Massieu ignored him so d'Estivet made a point of standing between them and the doors of the chapel when they passed so that Joan could not see the Host or say her prayers there.

Day Two of the trial began at 8 a.m. with the same struggle over the oath. Joan stuck to her refusal to take a blanket oath to tell the truth as she said she did not

---

[9] Pernoud, p. 170

know in advance what they would ask her. Again, she agreed to a strictly limited oath. Questions proceeded about the beginning of her mission, her relations with Baudricourt and the journey to Chinon to see the Dauphin.

A copy of her letter to the English Duke of Bedford was read out and she disputed some of the wording saying that it had been changed.

Then the questions turned to her voices and she refused to answer. She simply replied, 'Pass over that'. This was a phrase her judges were to hear often.

At this session, another attempt was made to control what was recorded of the trial. Manchon, whose job it was to record the trial, reported later at Joan's Trial of Rehabilitation that Cauchon commanded two clerics to hide in an alcove behind a heavy curtain near the judges and write down what was said. Manchon and his fellow notary sat in front of the judges officially recording the trial.

Manchon recalled that the two hidden clerics wrote while Joan spoke but they only recorded things that could be used against her. They did not record any of her explanations or answers that would have been favourable to her defence. Loiselleur (the treacherous priest who had already tricked Joan by visiting her in her cell and pretending to be on her side, even hearing her confession) was hidden with them to keep an eye on what they wrote. After dinner, Manchon recalled, they all met at Cauchon's house for a collation of their records. As the two clerks reported things differently from Manchon, Cauchon became very angry with Manchon and attempted to get him to change his record to agree with the others. He maintained that he had recorded what he had heard and refused to change it. The next day, Joan was questioned again about the points where the clerks had differed in their recordings and her replies confirmed the accuracy of what Man-chon had written.

# Chapter 43: One at a Time, Please

Between February 22 and March 3, there were five public sessions. They began at 8 a.m. and finished at 11 a.m. Joan sat facing the assembled churchmen. Often several of them put questions at the same time and interrupted her answers.

At one stage she said: 'Good gentlemen, one after the other.'

At another time, two of her questioners were asking her questions simultaneously. Joan told them she did not want to reply to so many questions at once.

'You do me great injustice to torment me like this. I have already replied on all these matters.'

Jean Beaupère, a man who had no sympathy whatsoever for Joan, was leading the questioning at one particular session. Even he became tired of the constant interruptions and angrily told his colleagues: 'Let her speak! It is I who have the job of interrogating her.'

Over and over again, the questions returned to the nature of the voices she heard. In the midst of one such interrogation session, Joan suddenly turned to Cauchon.

'You say you are my judge,' she said, 'Take care as to what you do for in truth I am sent from God and you are putting yourself in great danger.'

Later in the same session, she was presented with a question designed to trap her. She was asked: 'Do you believe you are in a state of grace?' If she admitted she was not in a state of grace, she was denying her claim to be sent by God. If she said she was in a state of grace, she would be claiming to know the mind of God on the subject. She could not win either way.

One of the assessors, Jean Le Fèvre, spoke out at the unfairness of the question, saying that Joan was not bound to answer such a huge question.

He was ignored. In the silence that followed, more than one hundred learned Churchmen waited breathlessly for the answer of an unschooled farm girl.

Joan replied: 'If I am not, may God put me in it; and if I am, may God keep me in it.'

All present were stunned at the brilliance of it. Cauchon was beside himself. He turned on Jean Le Fèvre and shouted: 'You, you would have done better to keep silent!'

During the public sessions, questions were asked about her male dress, her sword, her banner, and her prediction that she would be wounded at Orléans.

She was asked, 'At the coronation in the cathedral in Reims, was your banner waved around the King's head?'

'No,' she replied, 'It was not.'

'Why was it that your standard had a place at the coronation of the King rather than those of the other captains?'

Joan raised her head and her eyes were bright. 'It had borne the burden. It had earned the honour.'

But again, and again, the questions came back to her voices. On the 27 February, she admitted that her voices had spoken to her only a few days earlier.

In one session the questioning went as follows:

'Does Saint Margaret speak English?'

Joan replied, 'Why should she speak English as she is not on the English side?'

'What did Saint Michael look like when he appeared to you?'

'I did not see any crown and I know nothing about his garments.'

'Was he naked?'

Joan saw the humour in this and replied, 'Do you think our Lord has nothing to dress him in?'

'Had he any hair?'

Again Joan responded, 'Why should it have been cut off?'

They tried another trap. She was asked if Saint Margaret and Saint Catherine hated the English.

Joan replied simply, 'They love that which our Lord loves, and hate that which God hates.'

On another occasion she was asked if she had been in a place where the English were killed.

She replied impatiently, 'In God's name yes. How gently you talk! Why don't they leave France and go back to their own country?'

In the audience, was a high ranking English Lord who was so moved by this burst of patriotism he remarked: 'Really, this is a fine woman! If only she were English.'

Although she was exhausted, sometimes ill, harassed and alone, Joan did not show fear or awe of the great men confronting her. Her responses were often said jokingly. She caught out notary Boisguillaume who had recorded one of her responses eight days earlier. Her memory was better than his even though he had written it down. She told him jokingly in front of the whole court if he made such a mistake again, she would pull his ears.

While they returned again and again to the same questions, it was the subject of her male dress that they began to home in on. Joan had explained over and over that she wore male outfits at the command of her voices so that, given the circumstances she moved in, she was less likely to be raped than if she wore a woman's dress. Conducting a medieval military campaign both on and off a horse, in a full length skirt would also appear impractical.

They resorted to the laws of an ancient Hebrew tribe and quoted Deuteronomy in the Old Testament, Chapter XXII. 'The woman shall not wear that which pertaineth unto a man'. On the subject of her cropped hair, they fell back on Saint Paul in the New Testament, I Corinthians xi where he maintained that women should not only cover their heads but should also wear their hair long.

Joan maintained that it was by God's command that she dressed as she did and if he commanded her to wear some other form of clothing, she would do it.

She had asked to hear Mass and had been denied it. She was asked: 'Since you ask to hear Mass, would it not be more seemly to hear it in woman's clothes? Would you rather take woman's clothes and hear Mass or retain man's clothes and not hear it?

Joan replied: 'Guarantee that I shall hear it if I dress as a woman, and then I will answer.'

Throughout the trial, everyone was very impressed by Joan's ability to remember answers she had given days and weeks before. As already mentioned, she had

On 18 March, the assessors called a halt for a week and assembled in Cauchon's house to review the evidence so far. On 24 March they were back in the cell with the prisoner and there they read the documents of the trial to her in French. She acknowledged it all as a true record of what she had said.

The next day was Palm Sunday and she asked repeatedly to be allowed to hear Mass. She asked again on Easter Sunday. On both occasions she was asked if she would give up her male clothing and dress as a woman if they let her attend Mass. She replied that she had not been told by her counsel to give up the male dress. They then told her to get guidance from her counsel but she said it was not in her to do so. She begged to hear Mass, saying that the male clothing did not oppress her soul and she should be able to hear Mass dressed as she was.

Seventy items or articles were drawn up detailing her offences and on 27 March, she was brought back to the hall to hear them. Cauchon assured her that the wise and learned doctors did not want vengeance or physical punishment. All they wanted, he said, was to bring her back into the way of truth and salvation. He said they would allow her to choose one or more from among the assessors to be her adviser.

As Joan scanned the faces of the men before her, men who had been persecuting her in public and in private, she answered with courtesy and dignity.

'In the first place, I thank you in so far as you admonish me for my good. As to the counsel you offer me, I thank you also, but I have no intention of forsaking the counsel of our Lord.'

The reading of the seventy articles continued on the next day, 28 March. Three days later Cauchon and several others visited Joan in her cell and tried to persuade her to revoke her words and beliefs. She refused.

The seventy articles were then refined down to twelve and each of the assessors was given a copy and asked to deliver his opinion within a week. By 12 April, all the responses were in Cauchon's hands. All agreed on the verdict – heretic.

On 18 April, Cauchon and the inner circle visited Joan again. She had been very ill and she herself thought she might be dying. She requested that she be allowed confession and communion and that she be buried in consecrated ground. They told her that if she would not obey the Church they would abandon her as a Saracen, a heathen. She replied that she would put her trust in God.

She did not die. On 2 May another sitting was held in the hall rather than the prison. Sixty-five of them were present. The Archdeacon of Evreaux, Jean de Chatillon, was to deliver a sermon. Before Joan was brought in, Cauchon addressed them, beseeching them to do everything possible to bring the straying lamb back into the fold. Joan was sent for and the Archdeacon delivered his sermon. It was along the lines of the evils of new things beyond our understanding and the wisdom of respecting the old ways.

They resorted to threatening her, telling her she would be burnt if she continued with her heresy. She replied: 'I will say no more about that. Were I to see the fire, I would still say all that I have said, and would not do otherwise.'

They talked about her clothes, her attitude to the Pope, the sign she had given to the King which she repeatedly refused to tell them about.

They asked her if any of her supporters were brought there under safe conduct, would she tell them the things she had refused to talk about at the trial.

She replied, 'Do you think you can catch me by these means and thus win me to you?'

She asked for time to consider her final answer and they gave her a week. On 8 May, the second anniversary of the day she had relieved the siege of Orléans, she was taken to another tower in the castle, to face a handful of her judges and assessors. Here she was shown the instruments of torture which they were ready to use on her.

'Truly,' she said, 'even if you were to tear my limbs asunder and drive my soul out of my body, I could not speak otherwise; and, if I did say anything, I should always say afterwards that you had forced me to it.'

This wasn't the answer her accusers were expecting. Cauchon ordered her to be taken back to her prison cell.

Three days later, he called a conference of twelve of his colleagues at his house. They discussed the use of torture and then voted on it. The decision was made, ten to three, not to use torture. Those voting against it considered it unnecessary in this case and serving no purpose. The three who wanted to have Joan tortured were Aubert Morel, Thomas de Courcelles and Nicholas Loiselleur.

Following this meeting, Cauchon went to Paris to report the decision to the University of Paris and returned three days later with their response. They declared unanimously that, unless Joan retracted her statements, she was damned as a heretic, sorceress, destructive of the unity of the Church (schismatic) and guilty of abandoning the Faith (apostate).

It was decided to make one more effort to convince Joan to renounce her beliefs and retract her statements. On 23 May 1431, the twelve charges were read and explained to her. Again she refused to retract.

# Chapter 45: Choose the Fire

The next day, Joan was taken to the walled cemetery in Rouen where two stands had been erected. On one, stood her judges and numerous other important people. On the other, Joan was placed with Guillaume Erard, the preacher who was to give a sermon. The crowd was enormous and very excited, pushing and jostling to see the prisoner in chains, still dressed as a boy. Erard began his sermon using the text of the Gospel of St John: the branch cannot bear fruit of itself, except it abide in the vine …'

Halfway through his sermon, he changed tack and, speaking in a loud voice, proclaimed: 'Ah, France, you have been much abused and Charles, who calls himself your King and ruler, has endorsed the words and deeds of this useless, infamous, and dishonoured woman, like the heretic and schismatic that he is; and not he only, but all his clergy, by whom she has been examined and not rebuked.' He repeated these words two or three times then, pointing his finger at Joan, he said: 'I am speaking to you Joan and tell you that your King is a heretic and a schismatic.'

This was the King who made absolutely no effort to ransom or negotiate or save Joan to whom he owed his crown; this was the King who remained passive and aloof while Joan was set up for slaughter.

But Joan's loyalty to Charles did not waver. She could not let Erard's insults to Charles go unanswered and she interrupted him.

'By my faith, I dare to say and to swear on my life that he is the most noble of all Christians, who best loves the faith and the Church and is not as you say.'

'Tell her to be quiet!' Erard snapped at Massieu who had escorted Joan to the stand.

He then told her to submit her words and deeds to the Church.

She answered him 'As for my submission to the Church, I have already given them my answer. Let all my words and deeds be sent to Rome, to our Holy Father the Pope, to whom, after God, I will refer myself. As to what I have said and done, I have done it through God. I charge no one, neither my King nor any other; if there is any fault, it is mine alone.'

She was told that this was not enough, the Pope was too far away and her judges had the right to try her. She did not reply and Cauchon began to read the sentence of execution.

Joan listened to his pronouncements. The cruel crowd pushed forward eagerly to hear and to see. The executioner stood ready with his cart to take her away. It was finally too much for her. She gave way and declared she would surrender to the Church and her judges and she would no longer believe her voices.

The crowd went wild. The noise and confusion surrounded the prisoner and stones were thrown. One of the secretaries produced a small prepared document and a pen and gave it to Joan to sign.

She said: 'I know neither how to read nor write.'

The secretary insisted and she took the pen and drew a round 'O'. This was a mark she had used in the past to indicate that she did not agree with what was written. The secretary took her hand and forced her to make another mark. Possibly a cross.

Witnesses at the event said that the document Joan signed was about six to eight lines of large writing. The copy written into the official proceedings is some fifty lines of small writing and is an appalling confession of wrong doing.

It was now necessary to change the sentence. Joan had recanted. She had saved herself from the fire. She was sentenced to life imprisonment instead. She expected to be placed in a prison run by the Church and to be free of the English guards and their constant harassment.

She called out to the French Churchmen: 'Take me to your prison that I may no longer be in the hands of these English."

But Cauchon turned to the guards and said: 'Take her back to the place you brought her from.'

The English were furious that she had escaped burning. They taunted and insulted her as she was led away. The English captains did nothing to stop the harassment. The English noblemen surged around Cauchon threatening him with their swords and accusing him of not earning the money they had paid him to burn the witch.

Joan was taken back to her cell, chained to her block of wood with three English guards in the cell and two outside.

She was distraught. Her physical situation was bad enough but mentally she was in torment. She had betrayed her voices or had they betrayed her? Her thoughts were interrupted by five visitors – Lemaistre,

Loiselleurs, de Courcelles, Nicolas Midi and Isambard de la Pierre.

They told her that God and they had been extremely merciful and made it clear that any further relapse would give her no further chance of redemption. They then demanded that she put on a woman's dress. She did so. They shaved her head, a common punishment to humiliate a disgraced woman. Then they left her.

Imagine Cauchon's surprise to hear later that Joan had resumed male dress. She had ensured her own execution by doing so.

# Chapter 46: Trapped and Tricked

Massieu who had helped Joan as much as he dared as he escorted her to and from the trial and to the cemetery, spoke with Joan and asked her why she had gone back on her word and put on the male clothes. Joan told him the story.

'When I put on the woman's dress, my male clothes were put into a sack and left in the cell. One morning I woke up and asked the guards to free me from my chains so that I could relieve myself. One of the soldiers took the female clothes from me and emptying the male clothes from the sack, threw them on the bed. He then put the female dress into the sack and refused to give it to me. I reminded the guards that wearing male clothes was forbidden to me but nothing I said could persuade them to give me back the dress. I argued with them till noon but finally I had no choice but to put on the male clothes.'

Isambard de la Pierre recalled that when he saw her in prison, she was in great distress and outrage, her face wet with tears. She told him that since she had put on female clothes the harassment by the English guards had worsened. She told Ladvenu on her last morning alive that she had been sexually assaulted by an English nobleman.

When Cauchon heard she had resumed male clothes, he went to her cell to question her.

'Why do you dress as a man? Who has told you to dress as a man?' he shouted.

She replied: 'I took it of my own free will. No one constrained me to take it. … I prefer to dress as a man. … I think it safer to dress as a man when I am among men. I took it because you did not keep your word to me. You have not let me hear Mass, you have not taken me out of these chains, you have not put me in a decent prison with a woman to guard me. If you do these things, I will do whatever the Church wants."

'Since your abjuration have you heard the voices of Saints Catherine and Margaret?' Cauchon asked.

'Yes,' said Joan.

'What did they say to you?'

'They told me that through them God sent me his pity and that I did wrong to betray them to save my life. It was fear of the fire that made me say what I did.'

This was the fatal answer.

When Cauchon left Joan, he told the waiting Englishmen, "Farewell, be of good cheer, it is done!"

# Chapter 47: Death!

The next day, Tuesday 29 May, forty-one of the assessors met with Cauchon and voted unanimously. The decision: relapsed heretic. Joan was to be handed over to the secular authorities to be burnt.

Wednesday, 30 May 1431 dawned clear and bright.

Massieu who had defied Cauchon by allowing Joan to pray outside the chapel, was with her on this the last day of her life. He stayed with her to the end and it is from his record of that day that we know what happened.

It was the priest Ladvenu's duty to tell Joan her fate and Massieu and a monk named Toutmouillé went with him.

The two English guards posted outside the cell barely acknowledged them. They had seen the priests come and go often enough. Inside the cell were four other guards.

'Leave us with the prisoner,' Ladvenu said to them. 'I will hear her confession.'

Sullenly they left, casting suggestive leers at her. She ignored them.

She was dressed in a black shift with a handkerchief tied over her shaven head. She was chained by the waist to a heavy block of wood, as she had been for many months. She looked exhausted.

Ladvenu turned to Massieu. 'Get Cauchon's permission to give her Communion,' he said.

This was a surprise as Cauchon, had forbidden this for months although Joan had repeatedly requested it.

Massieu did as he was told and went to Cauchon to get his permission.

This took some time as a number of people had to be called together to make a decision. Finally permission was granted and a clerk came with the Sacraments. Ladvenu and Massieu were not pleased with the lack of ceremony and sent the clerk away to get candles and the proper stole to cover the Sacrament.

Joan received communion as Massieu says 'with great devotion and many tears'.

Then it was Ladvenu's unpleasant duty to tell her how she was to die. She had always had a horror of fire and she broke down and cried. She looked at the three men with terror in her eyes.

'Alas, that I should be treated so horribly and cruelly; that my whole body, never yet corrupted, should today be consumed and burnt to ashes! Oh, I would rather be beheaded seven times, than thus be burnt.'

At this moment, Cauchon and Pierre Maurice entered the cell and she turned to Cauchon: 'Bishop, I die through you.'

Cauchon stared at her. 'You!' he roared. 'You heretic. You dress like a boy. You have broken your promise not to wear men's clothing. You prefer to listen to the voices of saints rather than the wisdom of the Churchmen. You have brought this on yourself.'

She replied that if he had put her into a Church prison with suitable guards, this would never have happened.

Then turning to Maurice she asked: 'Maitre Pierre, where shall I be tonight?'

He asked her: 'Do you not trust in God?'

'Yes, I do,' she answered. 'God willing, I will be in Paradise.'

Then they led her out. Some eighty English soldiers were waiting for her, armed with swords, axes and sticks. They would let no one speak with her except Massieu and Ladvenu who kept close to her. Both men were in tears. Isambard de la Pierre followed close behind them.

In the market place of Rouen, stands had been built, one for the judges, one for the priests and one for a stake piled high with wood. The stake was inserted into a high plaster base, high enough so that no one would miss the agony of Joan of Arc. It was 9 a.m. and already some ten thousand people were waiting to watch her die.

Joan was put into the executioner's cart. Loiselleur, who had done so much to persecute her, was now struck by the reality of what he had helped bring about. Tears streamed down his face. He tried to climb into the cart to ask her forgiveness but the English attacked him and chased him away.

Martin Ladvenu and Jean Massieu stayed close by Joan's side. She was in tears with the horror of what lay ahead of her but there was nothing they could do to comfort her.

The cart was taken out of the castle through a small gate on the west side then continued through the narrow streets to the Old Market Place. We can hardly imagine the feelings of the nineteen-year old girl as she entered the market place – the eager crowd, the judges and priests on their platforms and the stake awaiting her. Nailed to the stake was a sign which read:

*Joan, who had herself called the Maid, liar, pernicious deceiver of the people, sorceress, superstitious, blasphemer of God, defamer of the faith of Jesus Christ, boastful, idolatrous, cruel, dissolute, invoker of demons, apostate, schismatic and heretic.*

Joan was made to mount the platform with the priest so everyone could see her. The priest, Nicolas Midi, began his sermon which went on for a very long time. Joan stood and listened without a word. When the sermon finally finished, Cauchon stood up and read the Church's sentence which cast out from the protection of the Faith and handed her over to the secular authorities.

Joan knelt down and began to pray. She asked pardon of her judges, the English, the King of France and all the princes of the kingdom. She asked that they would pray for her, saying that she forgave them all the harm they had done her. By the end of it the judges and even some of the English were in tears.

Knowing what was to come, Manchon the trial recorder left the scene. Her old enemy, Loiselleur, also left still in tears.

No secular sentence was pronounced, English soldiers grabbed her and hoisted her up on the scaffold. A mitre was placed on her head with the words: *Heretic, relapsed, apostate, idolator*, written on it.

Massieu and Ladvenu climbed up on the scaffold with her and she begged for a crucifix. An English soldier made her a little cross from two pieces of wood and handed it up to Massieu. Joan took the little makeshift cross, kissed it and placed it inside her gown on her breast. Isambard la Pierre and the parish priest ran to the nearest church to get the crucifix. Returning with it, la Pierre climbed up on the scaffold and held the crucifix in front of Joan.

She told him: 'When the fire is lit, get down but hold the cross up so I can still see it.'

She was chained to the stake and her hands were tied. She called out to Saint Catherine, Saint Margaret and Saint Michael. Some of the English began to laugh at her.

'Rouen, Rouen, I have great fear that you will suffer for my death,' she cried.

Massieu remained beside her, still trying to comfort her. The English became impatient and began to call out: 'Well, priest, do you mean us to dine here?'

Massieu was forced to climb down. The fire was lit and the flames engulfed her.

The executioner later reported that Joan's death had been exceptionally cruel. The scaffold had been built so high that he could not climb up to kill her quickly as was the custom. He had been forced to let her die in the fire. She was heard calling the name of Jesus again and again. They were her last words.

The English then ordered the executioner to push back the fire so everyone could see her naked burnt body hanging from the stake. They wanted to be sure no rumours of her escape could be circulated later. Others wanted to see that she was indeed a woman as they did not believe a woman could have accomplished the things she did.

The fire was then stirred up again and her body burnt to ashes.

*Joan's death.*
*Sculpture on the pedestal of the statue in Orléans.*

It is hard to imagine this final indignity occurring if the victim had been male. Joan of Arc who had sworn herself to chastity, who had dressed in male clothes so as not to stir sexual feelings in the soldiers she fought and slept with, had kept her body pure for God. At the end of her young life, the crowd was invited to gaze upon her naked corpse.

The executioner later went looking for Ladvenu and la Pierre. He was in a state of shock with fear and guilt.

'I have burned a saint,' he cried to them. 'God will never forgive me.' He told them that in spite of all the oil, sulphur and fuel he had used, he had been unable to reduce her heart and entrails to ash and had thrown them into the Seine.

She was only nineteen.

# SECTION 11: AFTERWARDS

I returned to Domremy and sat on the remains of the stone wall near the house of Joan's parents. My legs covered the plaque designating this as the place where she had first heard those voices. I looked across at the house, surprisingly modern in its design. Her parents were not poor or simple if the house was anything to go by.

A soft voice brought me back to my mission. "A penny for your thoughts." Joan peeped around the tree beside me. I stood up as she walked towards me.

She was wearing a simple page boy's outfit, all one colour, just as on that first day I had seen her. Again, I thought it was black but as she moved, I realised it was a rich deep maroon. Her black hair was still cut in a thick page boy bob. Her face glowed and her eyes sparkled. It was the happiest I had seen her.

She motioned for me to sit back on the wall and sat beside me, her soft shoes resting halfway up the rock face. Her elbows rested on her knees, her chin in her hands. She was like a child again.

I couldn't resist the question:

'Do you come here often?'

She saw the humour of it but chose to answer seriously.

'Actually, no. I was drawn to you that first time in the church but I haven't re-visited any of the places of my – what shall I call it – earthly life, very much.'

The sparkle left her eyes briefly but she quickly regained her good humour. I was relieved to see her after our experience in Rouen so I got straight down to business.

'Joan, there are still so many questions left to ask you. Are you aware of the things that happened after you were burned?'

She nodded, 'Some of it,' she said.

I continued. 'For example, what happened to your mission to drive the English out of France? What, if anything, did your King DO? What happened to your parents, what about your brothers especially Pierre who was captured with you? '

'Hold on, one at a time, one at a time!' she interrupted.

We both laughed remembering the way her judges had thrown so many questions at her at once and how she had replied as politely as she could: "Good gentlemen, one after the other."

'Where would you like to start,' she asked.

'Tell us about Pierre. He rode with you for the whole of your campaigning and he was captured with you at Compèigne. What happened to him after that?'

'Pierre was imprisoned by the Burgundians not the English and was treated in the usual manner. That is, he was held for ransom and, when the ransom was paid, he was freed. I told you already that Charles had granted my whole family the name *du Lys* and the right to a coat of arms with French lilies and a sword. He and my brother Jean both adopted that name.

Pierre did marry. His first wife died and he married a second time.

'Pierre looked after Mama too because Father died not long after I did. Mama went to Orléans to live and Pierre went with her. I don't know what happened to his wife and children. Mama was the driving force behind my rehabilitation and Pierre helped her with that. I have to admit that my King saw the wisdom of rehabilitating the person responsible for getting him crowned. Leaving me with those charges against me would have also challenged his legitimacy to the Crown. Mama died in 1458 and Pierre died soon after. He was a good brother to me in difficult circumstances most brothers never experience.'

I thought that was an understatement but said nothing.

She continued, 'I heard the French finally drove the English out but it took another couple of decades. Our King Charles had a very capable mother-in-law, Yolande of Anjou and she organized to have very good advisers appointed to court. That's why in later years Charles was called "The Well Served".

'Yes,' I said, 'And the French army began to use guns and gunpowder very effectively instead of relying so much on men on horseback charging about. Your old friend Dunois, the Bastard of Orléans did quite a bit of damage to the English side using artillery. Also your King Charles reformed the army and gradually eliminated all the marauding bands and scavengers that acted independently as small armies of France. And you'll be pleased to hear that Richemont got back to his rightful position as Constable of France and finally managed to get rid of that scheming Trémoille from the court.'

Joan looked amazed. 'Good for Artur,' she said, referring to Richemont.

'Richemont was the one who recovered Paris from the enemy and he also put down a revolt of the nobles when they didn't like Charles disbanding their independent little armies. He certainly served Charles well. As did you,' I added. 'Charles didn't do anything to save you or ransom you. He just let you die. When the English were almost driven out of the country, he decided to do something about you. He realized that by declaring you a heretic and sorceress, the English had cast doubt on his own legitimacy again since it was you who succeeded in getting him crowned.

'Eighteen years after your death, in December 1449, he entered the city of Rouen. It had been occupied by the enemy for thirty years. He set up a hearing into your death and called seven mostly friendly witnesses. They were Ladvenu and Isambard le la Pierre, Manchon and Massieu, all of whom I recall did their best to help you in one way or another during your trial and execution. There were also Toutmouille and Guillaume Duval who had been present at your trial. The only hostile witness was Jean Beaupère. He was the one who asked you that question about being in a state of grace. The process declared your original trial prejudicial and void. It didn't mean much though since you'd been tried by the Inquisition and only the Inquisition could reverse it.'

Joan took up the story. 'I heard about this bit. In November 1455, the Pope initiated a hearing in Paris. Mama was brought from Orléans by my brother Pierre and gave the opening statement in the Cathedral of Notre Dame de Paris. Like me, she faced an all-male assembly, but unlike me she was not alone, thank goodness. She was surrounded by supporters and well-wishers and Pierre was with her.

'To be honest, this rehabilitation trial was as biased as the first one but in the opposite direction. Where Cauchon disallowed the inclusion of anything that supported me, this trial skipped over things that might have gone against me. My male clothes, my short hair, my refusal to accept the authority of the Churchmen over my voices. All the things the first trial condemned me for. Many witnesses were called to testify on my behalf. The first trial was formally declared prejudicial and improper. In July 1456, the documents of condemnation and the sentence from my first trial were burnt in the Old Market Place in Rouen. The same place they'd burnt me. Didn't do me much good though.

'Mama died two years later at least with the limited satisfaction that the charges against me had been reversed and, as I said before, my brother, Pierre, died not long after Mama.'

"You know they made you a saint,' I said.

'I'd heard. As you know it was two saints and an archangel who got me into this in the first place and you and I both know I wasn't all that saintly. Tell me how it happened.'

'Well in 1869, your name was put forward for consideration along with the name of Christopher Columbus. You know, the man who first took Christianity to the Americas. At least, that's why he was being considered for sainthood. But they found he was the father of an illegitimate son so that disqualified him. Your case was argued on and off for fifty years because you weren't exactly the Church's most obedient daughter. Finally, in 1920, they made you a saint.'

'Poor Christopher,' she said then added. 'I've enjoyed talking to you but it's time for me to go. *Adieu mon amie*. Thank you.'

I reached out to touch her but she was gone. I'll never forget you,' I whispered.

# Bibliography

There are hundreds of books about Joan of Arc and masses of information on the Internet.

The following are a selection of books I have found helpful or inspiring.

KENEALLY, THOMAS. *Blood Red, Sister Rose.* Book Club Associates, Sydney, 1974

LUCIE-SMITH, EDWARD. *Joan of Arc,* Penguin Books, London, 2000.

PERNOUD, REGINE. *Joan of Arc.* Scarborough House, 1994.

SACKVILLE-WEST, VITA. *Saint Joan of Arc.* Penguin, 1955.

SHAW, BERNARD. *Saint Joan.* Penguin Books, Mitcham, Vic. 1955

TWAIN, MARK. *Joan of Arc.* Ignatius Press, San Francisco, 1989

WARNER, MARINA. *Joan of Arc.* University of California Press, 1981.

WILSON-SMITH, TIMOTHY. *Joan of Arc.* Sutton Publishing, 2006.

# Index

LaVergne, TN USA
15 February 2011
216569LV00001B/21/P